CAMBRIDGE LIBRARY COLLECTION

Books of enduring scholarly value

Cambridge

The city of Cambridge received its royal charter in 1201, having already been home to Britons, Romans and Anglo-Saxons for many centuries. Cambridge University was founded soon afterwards and celebrated its octocentenary in 2009. This series explores the history and influence of Cambridge as a centre of science, learning, and discovery, its contributions to national and global politics and culture, and its inevitable controversies and scandals.

A Short History of Newnham College, Cambridge

To mark the fiftieth anniversary of the foundation of Newnham College, the second Cambridge college to offer university education to women, its Council asked Alice Gardner to write this short history, published in 1921. Gardner (1854–1927) had gone up to Newnham in 1876: she had achieved the highest history degree in her year (though she was not allowed to graduate), and went on to a distinguished teaching career in Cambridge and Bristol. The book describes 'the idea of Newnham', which arose from supporters of female education in the mid-nineteenth century, the parallel trajectory of the founders of Girton College, and the small beginning of what became Newnham, with five students in a house overlooking Parker's Piece in 1871. Gardner takes the story up to 1914 (with a short epilogue), ending with the hypothesis, 'If Newnham ever becomes a College of the University …', a status eventually achieved in 1948.

Cambridge University Press has long been a pioneer in the reissuing of out-of-print titles from its own backlist, producing digital reprints of books that are still sought after by scholars and students but could not be reprinted economically using traditional technology. The Cambridge Library Collection extends this activity to a wider range of books which are still of importance to researchers and professionals, either for the source material they contain, or as landmarks in the history of their academic discipline.

Drawing from the world-renowned collections in the Cambridge University Library and other partner libraries, and guided by the advice of experts in each subject area, Cambridge University Press is using state-of-the-art scanning machines in its own Printing House to capture the content of each book selected for inclusion. The files are processed to give a consistently clear, crisp image, and the books finished to the high quality standard for which the Press is recognised around the world. The latest print-on-demand technology ensures that the books will remain available indefinitely, and that orders for single or multiple copies can quickly be supplied.

The Cambridge Library Collection brings back to life books of enduring scholarly value (including out-of-copyright works originally issued by other publishers) across a wide range of disciplines in the humanities and social sciences and in science and technology.

A Short History of Newnham College, Cambridge

Alice Gardner

CAMBRIDGE
UNIVERSITY PRESS

CAMBRIDGE
UNIVERSITY PRESS

University Printing House, Cambridge, CB2 8BS, United Kingdom

Cambridge University Press is part of the University of Cambridge.

It furthers the University's mission by disseminating knowledge in the pursuit of
education, learning and research at the highest international levels of excellence.

www.cambridge.org
Information on this title: www.cambridge.org/9781108082631

This edition first published 1921
This digitally printed version 2015

ISBN 978-1-108-08263-1 Paperback

A SHORT HISTORY OF
NEWNHAM COLLEGE, CAMBRIDGE

PUBLISHERS.

CAMBRIDGE.

LONDON: MACMILLAN & CO., LIMITED
GLASGOW: MACLEHOSE, JACKSON & CO.

By Mrs F W H Myers

Henry Sidgwick

A SHORT HISTORY
OF
NEWNHAM COLLEGE
CAMBRIDGE

BY

ALICE GARDNER, M.A. (Bristol)

FORMERLY LECTURER AND FELLOW OF NEWNHAM COLLEGE, CAMBRIDGE
AUTHOR OF "THE LASCARIDS OF NICÆA," "THEODORE OF STUDIUM," ETC.

WITH TEN ILLUSTRATIONS

CAMBRIDGE
BOWES & BOWES
1921

TO THE HONOURED MEMORY
OF A. J. C. AND H. S.

PREFACE

THIS little book is primarily intended for present and past students of Newnham College and for the numerous friends who have been helpers or sympathetic spectators of its early progress. At the same time I venture to hope that it may prove interesting and suggestive to a wider circle of persons practically or theoretically concerned in movements for the higher education of women.

Of the deficiencies of this short history, no one could be more fully aware than the writer herself. But for the expressed wish of the Council of Newnham College, it would never have been attempted, nor could it have been written at all without the kind co-operation of friends, who, like myself, had known the College from the inside. I would especially thank the present Principal, Miss B. A. Clough, and the Registrar, Miss E. M. Sharpley, for supplying me with information and with kindly criticisms throughout my task. It has been gratifying to realize that the Publisher is son of an early friend of the College.

One of the chief difficulties in writing the history of a comparatively young institution, and one raised

by the labours, forethought, and sacrifices of many
" pious founders and benefactors " is that the range
of view possible to any former student and teacher
must necessarily be limited. I have felt deep regret
in realizing how many honoured helpers have—for
lack of space—not even been mentioned. Similarly,
among the former students whose labours, scientific,
literary, and practical, have brought credit to the
College, I have necessarily shown most appreciation
of those with whose work and influence I have been
personally best acquainted. Every past student will
have to supplement the story with recollections from
her own experience.

I trust that, at least, I shall have brought home
to many the conviction that Newnham College is
unique, in the character and motives of its first
founders, in the steady devotion to its best interests
of successive governors, teachers and students, as
also in its relations—complicated, but near, we may
hope, to a solution—with the University under the
protecting shadow of which it has grown to prosperity. My hope for this little work is that, besides
helping to justify the existence of the College in the
eyes of the world, it may in some measure preserve
in its members the knowledge of our best traditions
in the past and inspire a confident hope for the future.

ALICE GARDNER.

BRISTOL, *April*, 1921.

CONTENTS

LIST OF ILLUSTRATIONS

For permission to reproduce the two illustrations of
Professor Henry Sidgwick and Miss A. J. Clough thanks
are due to Mrs. F. W. H. Myers; also to Messrs. Bassano
for the use of their photographs of Miss B. A. Clough, Miss
Katharine Stephen and the general view of the College.

A SHORT HISTORY OF
NEWNHAM COLLEGE

CHAPTER I

INTRODUCTORY. NEWNHAM COLLEGE IN IDEA

In tracing the history of educational institutions
and of other foundations existing for the public
good, we find it necessary to distinguish those that
had and those that had not a definite beginning.
Some of our colleges and great schools have—so to
speak—sprung, adult and armed, from the brain
of their founder—or possibly from the conjoint
thoughts and efforts of a few generous and like-
minded patrons. Their birthdays are easily determined. Their continuity can be traced both in
material persistence and progress and in moral
and intellectual development and adaptation to
changing conditions. Others — and prominent
among them the subject of this sketch—came into
being so gradually that their length of days may be
variously calculated. To the past students of
Newnham College, the beginning seems to be most

naturally and fittingly associated with the day when a comparatively small dwelling house was first opened, in Cambridge, by Professor Sidgwick and a small group of friends, and placed under the wise and devoted care of Miss Clough, for the accommodation of a few young women who wished to give their time to serious study under the tuition of such University professors, lecturers, and private teachers as might be willing to further their desire for higher education.   Incorporation as a College was not to come for nine years, nor any measure of distinct recognition by the University for ten years.   But no Newnham woman would reckon our beginnings from 1880 or 1881.   An antiquarian spirit might fancy that the germs were in the room in Mr. Clay's garden, where lectures were first delivered to women students and others.   But student life and university instruction had for us its first embodiment in the little community of five, and their teachers and helpers, whose relations with Cambridge began in 1871.

This settlement of Miss Clough and the five students was the small beginning out of which grew an institution which many hundreds of women now regard with passionate loyalty, and which no opponents or doubters can venture to despise.   To understand its origin we need to go back a little and consider how and why the movement towards higher education for women was then beginning to take

MISS ANNE J. CLOUGH AND THE FIRST FIVE STUDENTS.

form, and why it came to be specially associated with Cambridge.

It would be partly true and partly false to regard the objects of those who practically founded Newnham College as identical with those of the leading champions of the political and legal rights of women. Of course, as might naturally be expected, many of those who, through breadth of sympathy and hatred of injustice, gave the greater part of their lives and energies to the removal of female disabilities, public and private, were very ready to respond to the demand for higher education for girls and women. One need only think (looking at the leaders of thought in the middle of last century) of John Stuart Mill (a benefactor to the Cambridge Lectures Association and to similar enterprises) with the philosophic school which he represented and led. The advocates of political liberty and those of higher education for women used to a large extent the same arguments, and the securing of one end favoured the prospects of the other. Those who held that women were on the eve of obtaining greater rights and responsibilities were bound to show sympathy with the cause of education ; they could quote the words of Samson Agonistes : " What were strength without a double share of wisdom ? Vast, unwieldy, burdensome." And on the other hand every movement made in the direction of sound education for women told in favour of opening spheres of usefulness and conceding rights as to property and personal liberty which uneducated women might possibly have abused. Among the earlier friends of Newnham, probably by far the larger number were warmly attached to the franchise movement, especially when it came within the range of practical politics. At the same time, advocates of higher education were unlikely to be possessed— as were a few excellent and high-minded women—by the idea of the suffrage as a panacea for all women's grievances or a necessary condition of any step towards social betterment. Necessity and common sense prescribed caution to the pioneers who were directing their efforts to obtain some measure of university education for women able to profit thereby.

And indeed there was nothing revolutionary in the movement towards higher education for women. True, the education of girls and women had not till then been considered an object to be sought on a large scale. But there had been educated and even learned women in England, in the days of the Renaissance and Reformation, though there can be little doubt that—in the higher circles, at least—a check came with the frivolities of the later Stuart court. But without going into uncertain historical details, it is noticeable that in the early part of the nineteenth century, such different persons as Sydney Smith and Mrs. Hannah More became eloquent advocates of more serious education for girls than they commonly received. The arguments of these and like-minded reformers were not thrown away. It is beyond question that in many parts of England, in early and middle Victorian days, there were high-minded, intellectual, and accomplished women conducting girls' schools on reasonable principles and with good mental and moral results ; and a good deal of the highest education in girls' schools was given by men—sometimes of considerable standing and ability. The position of a private governess was not remarkably dignified or lucrative (*vide* the experiences of the Brontes) ; but there were some such private teachers who did excellent and much appreciated work.

Still the course of a girl who had inward longings for intellectual culture was often hard ; and harder still was that of young women who had a liking for literature and art, combined with a distaste for unvaried domestic interests or social routine. The happiest were those who had sympathetic elder brothers at College, who could talk over their difficulties with them and recommend books. Such was eminently the position of Miss Clough herself. Her education—discursive and not without lacunae—had been a home education, her chief mentor an Oxford brother, whose mind and tone of character it is superfluous here to describe. It was in great part to help those who, like herself, had had aspirations after knowledge and culture, and who, unlike herself, had not always had sympathetic homes, that she and other pioneers in Cambridge desired to secure facilities of continuous study under the direction of capable and inspiring teachers.

It may be advisable to indicate briefly the different ways in which efforts were made to meet the existing wants, some of which led up to the goal of university education for women.[1]

(1) The first step was the establishment of larger and better schools, and provision for more advanced teaching. Queen's College, Harley Street, first presided over by F. D. Maurice, was founded in 1848 and is still at work ; Bedford College (now a College of London University) was founded in 1849 ; the North London Collegiate School and Cheltenham College (which both maintain their position as schools of first-rate standing) in 1850 and 1858. There were started, besides, some colleges expressly for women intending to become teachers (the Maria Grey, Home and Colonial, etc.). At present the need of some serious training in the art

[1] In this part of the subject, and indeed throughout my task, I am constantly indebted to the *Memoir of Anne J. Clough by her Niece, B. A. Clough*. This book ought to be familiar to all interested in educational movements, since Miss Clough, while most closely associated with the University side of the movement, was throughout her life collaborating with great sympathy and insight with those at work in other departments.

of teaching is widely recognised. In the early days of the Women's Education Movement, a young woman had often practically to choose between gaining more knowledge, and learning to make the most of the little which she had. This difficulty is now much diminished, if not entirely removed.

(2) But almost more important than the new foundations, started generally by private effort, was the successful attempt to secure some kind of government inspection of girls' schools and the synchronizing responsibility undertaken by the Universities of Oxford and Cambridge in admitting girls to the Local Examinations. In 1864, the Schools Inquiry Commission were requested to include in their task the inspection of Girls' Schools. The result was a revelation of superficiality, narrowness, and general inefficiency which awoke a portion at least of the educated public to the need of reform. The result of the new experiment (1865) of admitting girls to the Cambridge Senior and Junior examinations showed similar defects. Many generations of Newnham students have been amused to hear among the recollections revived at the annual Commemoration, how it was once seriously proposed to lower the standard of arithmetic to suit the capacity of the girls. Happily the suggestion was not followed. The notion that women cannot do hard sums was one of the " hasty generalizations "

as to the constitution of the female mind, " with the wrecks of which," it was afterwards said, " the whole shore has been strewn."

The deficiencies of the schools were largely due to the fact that no opportunities of education were available for intending teachers. The more enlightened schoolmistresses had to struggle against masses of prejudice, indifference and materialism in the minds of parents and of the public, and many of them were eager for improvement. In 1866, the Society of London Schoolmistresses was formed for mutual help and encouragement, and similar societies were established in various localities, which lent support to the efforts of well-wishers in the Universities and elsewhere.

(3) Then again there were early schemes for lectures to women in different parts of the country, and these have branched out and become more effectual than any measure for educational improvement among persons for whom residence at a university was impossible. Here, as in many regions, Miss Clough was a pioneer, and this branch of work brought about the connection of Cambridge with one side of the movement and led directly to the starting of what grew into Newnham College.

The body which accomplished the chief initial work in the matter of local lectures for women was " The North of England Council for improving the Education of Women." To the organization of this society, Miss Clough gave much thought and attention, especially in 1867 and the following years. It was formed from an amalgamation of societies having the same object, in Liverpool, Manchester, Sheffield, Leeds and Newcastle. Among Miss Clough's colleagues on this Council were Mr. (afterwards Canon) and Mrs. Butler, Mr. (now Lord) Bryce, Mr. F. W. H. Myers, and Mr. (afterwards Professor) James Stuart. It was Mr. Stuart who, after his experience in the North of England, proposed and brought about in 1873 the organization of local lectures by the Universities. It is needless to go into the history of the subsequent development of University Extension. Begun primarily in the interests of women, it was extended to meet the needs of busy men with free evenings, working people, and all who wished in their leisure to prolong their education and gain culture.

(4) The work of the North of England Council led to a further step in the early development of what I have called "Newnham College in Idea," viz. the founding of the Cambridge Higher Local Examination. The request for an examination for women over eighteen came from the Council and was supported on the ground that it was desirable to have a definite and intelligible test for teachers, with some means of giving system to the lecture movement as far as it affected women, and of directing the reading of girls who had left

school. It had originally features which became modified with changing principles of education. There was at first a group of subjects considered essential as the foundation of liberal education and optional groups, some of which candidates had to take in order to secure a certificate. In course of time the groups were increased in number and larger choice allowed while the necessarv preliminaries were diminished.

The examination was first held in 1869, when thirty-six candidates were examined in two centres.[1] As this examination was from the first supposed to be one the reading for which would prove interesting and profitable to adult women, it is not surprising that it should have been eagerly used by the advocates of university education for intending teachers as a test of fitness for real university study. Later it became one of the school examinations taken by girls in the upper forms, and when the Tripos examinations were opened to women certain portions were accepted in lieu of the Previous Examination. The connection between Newnham and the Higher Local Examination was maintained for many years, certain scholarships being always awarded on its results, though the multiplication of other facilities for university qualification has now loosened the tie. In the early days Newnham College owed much to the Syndicate for Local Lectures and

[1] *Memoir of A. J. Clough*, p. 130.

Examinations, and to the courtesy and devotion of the successive Secretaries (Rev. G. F. (Bishop) Browne and Dr. Keynes) and to the fostering care which they bestowed on the young movement.

Here an auxiliary agency may be mentioned which was of real service to young women desirous either of passing the new examination or simply of understanding how and what to read for their own benefit : the scheme of instruction by correspondence, started and kept vigorous for many years by the late Mrs. Peile, wife of the highly respected tutor and afterwards Master of Christ's College. Among the instructors by correspondence were many distinguished members of the University. The curricula were designed with a view to the requirements of the Higher Local Examination, but subjects were handled freely and suitable books were recommended. This last necessity was partly met by a loan library for women.

These steps were gradually leading up to a possible university education for women. At first sight, our beginnings may seem to have a non-academic and amateurish air. And part of what was accomplished in these early days would meet with scant approval from modern advocates of equal chances for women with men in learning and the learned professions. Inspection of schools by government is now by many regarded as a necessary evil. Popular courses of lectures without regular sequence or adaptation to the previous attainments of those who attend them suggest superficiality and lack of scientific method. Instruction by correspondence is by many associated with cram of the lowest sort. But to those who read the correspondence of the founders of these institutions, or whose memory carries them back to the days when they were not only novel but a very godsend to labourers at self-education, the whole movement wears a different aspect. All methods of imparting knowledge are apt to degenerate into tricks for hiding ignorance; even respect for universities and learned men may become mere toadyism. But the early forms, though now a little outworn, did indicate and partly supply a genuine need, and led on to even better things—especially to academic training and advanced study for women.

(5) The general movement towards university education, on the other hand, begins with the inauguration of a series of lectures in Cambridge itself, somewhat like that already started in the north, but wider in scope and capable of being continued for the instruction of women far beyond the educational standard prescribed by the Local Examinations. This had its beginning in a drawing-room meeting held in Prof. and Mrs. Fawcett's house, late in 1869.

If these beginnings seem less dignified than those of Colleges erected for students and organized from the first on University lines, it may be remarked that, after all, the beginnings of Newnham bear some analogy to those of the early European universities, including the English. Perhaps in all the greatest centres of learning there has been first the great teacher—then the scholars who flock to sit at his feet. Colleges and social student life and hostels and regulated grades of teachers and taught are an aftergrowth. So, we may say, the first Newnham students came to Cambridge because great teachers were there; it was not that suitable teachers came because the students had shown a demand for them or for collegiate houses and collegiate life. The university extension lecturers might be useful and stimulating missionaries of culture, but their greatest service was to kindle a desire to go and drink at the fountain-heads. The mountain could not come to Mahomet, but many touched by prophetic zeal might make all efforts to come to the mountain.

The first step taken as a result of the historic meeting referred to in Prof. and Mrs. Fawcett's house, was the formation of a society to be called *the Association for promoting the Higher Education of Women in Cambridge.*

The first executive consisted of Mr. (afterwards Dr.) Bonney, Mr. (Dr.) Peile, Prof. F. D. Maurice, Mrs. Adams, Mrs. Bateson, Mrs. Fawcett, Mrs. Venn; the Secretaries were Mr. Markby and Mr. (afterwards

Professor) Henry Sidgwick ; the Treasurer Mrs.
Bateson.   Early in 1870, a list of lectures was
brought out.   Although these lectures were supposed
to be for women reading for the Higher (then called
the Women's) examination, they were given by men
generally of the highest standing in the University,
such as the university members of the Executive
just mentioned, besides Professor Skeat, Prof. J. E. B.
Mayor, Dr. Peile, Prof. Cayley, Dr. Venn, Mr.
Marshall and other eminent persons.   It may be
that some of these lecturers were decidedly " over
the heads " of such of the students as had had an
indifferent schooling and were only just commencing
adult study.   But the fault—if such we should call
it—was a good one.   As a rule, the partly self-taught
are more ready to grapple with difficulties than such
as have hitherto had the paths of progress made
gradual and easy ; and the very fact of being more
or less in contact with a master mind was rather
stimulating than depressing.

These lectures were originally given in a building
kindly lent by Mr. Clay, standing in the garden of
his house a little off Trumpington Street.

Besides the lectures specially arranged in connection with the new scheme, a large number of
lectures given by Professors of the University were,
by their special permission, opened to women.   In
those days the professorial lectures formed, generally
speaking, a less important part in the teaching of

the University than they do at present. This was not, of course, due to any inferiority in such lectures, but to the want of correlation in the instruction provided by the several colleges and by the University. As this correlation became more effectual, the privilege given to women students of attending professorial lectures became more and more advantageous to them. Twenty-eight professors acceded to the request of the Association, as well as two lecturers who delivered their lectures in University buildings. University Professors and Lecturers were, generally speaking, bound to admit all members of the University to their lectures without fee, but were allowed to charge fees to non-members. Women students came, of course, under the second head, but as a rule the Professors admitted them without fee, as if they were of undergraduate status. The gradual opening up of lectures given on the Intercollegiate system in the halls or lecture-rooms of the various colleges began, as will be seen, a little later.

But besides the special lectures to women and the professorial lectures provided for members of the University, a very necessary element in Cambridge teaching consists in private tuition—of students taken individually or in small groups In Classics and Mathematics, especially, such " coaching " is necessary both for backward and for advanced students. Among the earlier supporters of the

Women's Education movement were a good many brilliant teachers who, in their generous belief in the cause, were ready to give instruction to women students often in a far more elementary stage than the men they ordinarily taught. Fees were naturally paid to the private teachers, but in many cases, while the cause was yet poor and struggling, these fees were returned to the Treasurer.

The students who required the more advanced lectures and tuition were generally those who, having passed the Women's Examination, aimed at a real University course. Tripos students were among the very first generation of Cambridge women—though those who read with a view to triposes could never feel quite sure, till near the end of their three years, whether the examiners would think it consistent with their functions to admit women and declare what class they attained.

This great object had already been approached on independent lines by the founders of Girton College. Miss Davies had conceived hopes of founding an actual college in which the Cambridge degree examinations, pass and honour, might be taken by women, and in 1869 such a college was started at Hitchin. The intellectual ideals and standards of the two wings—so to speak—of the movement were not identical. Time and with it changes in the demands of the degree examinations at Cambridge—indeed at both Universities—have brought

MISS MARION KENNEDY.

them pretty close together. The very good reasons at the bottom of both programmes are easy to recognise. Miss Davies considered that any requirements made from women different from those demanded from men would certainly be lower. If women avoided Greek and the other subjects of which boys were supposed to learn something at school, an impression would be created that women were allowed graduate or quasi-graduate status on easier terms than those imposed on men. On the other side there was, in the minds of Sidgwick and others who became the founders of Newnham, a great contempt of the " Poll " as well as of the " Little-go " as marking a very low standard of intellectual achievement. At the same time, a more concrete mind like Miss Clough's deplored the inconvenience and waste of time which might keep an adult woman who had not learned classics or much mathematics at school, studying the beginnings of these subjects in school-boy fashion when her mind was more adapted to other studies. Again there was the fear—groundless enough as experience has proved—lest the girls' schools should be " classicized " and modern studies in them discouraged. In point of fact, Cambridge University now demands of candidates for the Previous Examinations only the very minimum of ancient languages, and the boys' schools have been de-classicized to a further extent than might have then

B

seemed possible. In the long run, the different
schemes proved to be very similar in results. The
Little-go Greek did no harm to those who took
it. Honestly taught (as, unfortunately, is not
always the case with a compulsory subject), it has
often given to the learner sufficient knowledge to
be of real service in later studies. A small amount
of rivalry at the outset has not hindered the progress
of the two Colleges side by side in co-operation and
mutual goodwill.

But before the first tripos student had definitely
entered on her career, another great step had been
taken : the opening of a house for the residence
of women who had been attracted by the educational
facilities of Cambridge and desired to devote
themselves there to some course of serious study.
The securing of a house for students had become
necessary in the eyes of Mr. Henry Sidgwick, and
foremost among the many and great services which
he rendered to the College (then hardly existing
even in idea) was that he persuaded Miss Clough to
come and take charge of the resident students.
A house was found in Regent Street, and in the
autumn of 1871 Miss Clough and five students
began their common life there, and initiated a new
stage in the movement.

Long years afterwards, when Newnham was large
and flourishing, with four Halls of residence, a large
party up for Commemoration met to explore the

cradle of this College, which was the more easily done as the house had become a hotel (The Bird Bolt Temperance Hotel). Two of the original five (Mrs. Marshall and Miss Larner) pointed out to the students of that day the one room which served as dining-room and as common study for these pioneer students; the other sitting-room used in the afternoon for lectures, overlooking Parker's Piece, where they, without a scrap of garden, could envy the boys playing on the Piece; the small rooms which were their bedrooms. The first generation had little elbow-room, no games, a scanty library, a non-luxurious *ménage*, and very little of what is now considered necessary freedom in work and play. Yet they seem to have been exceedingly happy. They felt, and the feeling remained for at least a dozen years, that they were pioneers. The lectures given by greater men than any they had ever seen before; the pleasures of intercourse, especially for those who had found little intellectual sympathy at home; the long walks over the Gogs or along the Cam, more enjoyed in pre-hockey, pre-bicycling, even pre-tennis days than now; the associations of an ancient and beautiful town; the sympathy shown by the generous men and women who had adopted their cause : all these things must far have outweighed the passing inconvenience of straitened accommodation and even the painful consciousness that the eye of the world and yet more of his wife was upon them, for better and for worse. But perhaps above all, in later days, these pioneer students felt most thankful to think that in that house they had enjoyed the constant presence of Miss Clough and frequent intercourse with the leaders of the movement, particularly of Mr. Henry Sidgwick.

It may seem superfluous as well as presumptuous for the present writer to dwell on the characteristics of the two leading persons in the early days of the College (or the college-embryo) seeing that their lives and characters have, as already said, been portrayed in biographies which are never likely to be surpassed. Perhaps, however, a little space may be given to those peculiarities which, in both characters, left a permanent impression on the College as a whole, especially since they exhibit traits of an almost opposite description, yet united to produce a great result. In one respect they were alike : in what may be called fundamental sincerity and whole-heartedness, along with wide ranges of interest. Readers of Sidgwick's life and writings cannot but be impressed with his absolute fidelity to any course which had shown itself worthy of approval, his careful attention to every opinion and principle which had any reasonable justification, his loyalty to personal convictions in avoiding any possible compromise with mental tergiversation. He had lately given up his fellowship from conscientious motives. He abstained from identifying himself with any form of institutional Christianity, while fully acknowledging how such Christianity had worked for good, and tolerating the attitude of those who were able for the sake of true religion to accept religious formulae with reservations of their own. In politics, he generally went with the more progressive Liberals, though fully able and always ready to grasp the situation of those who took different standpoints. The efforts and the personal sacrifices which he made in the cause of women's education were not inspired by any one-sided attachment to the cause either on a personal or on a theoretical side. He held no fixed theory as to the equality and similarity of the sexes in mental powers, but was in favour of assisting legitimate efforts, removing unreasonable limitations, and postponing the decision as to whether women *can* do this or that by giving them the opportunity and awaiting the result. When the result proved favourable to his reasoned expectations, he was naturally pleased, but on all subjects he ever kept an open mind. For persons handicapped in the race of life, by sex, nationality, or poverty, he was always ready to discover new prospects of successful effort. His family life had made him acquainted with women of exceptional gifts even before his marriage with Miss Eleanor Mildred Balfour in 1876, a happy event for Newnham as well as for himself. The frequent presence of a man of his calibre in the incipient college was of inestimable benefit to the early students. He was to them a champion of their cause and a model of sincerity and reasonableness, and to many a very helpful teacher. A larger proportion of students in the early days than later took up some branch of Moral Science—in which he directed their work. And to others he was helpful on the educational side by his encouragement of good literature— which may at times have tended to retreat into the background in favour of severely scientific study. Beyond all this there were traditions among the early students of his extraordinary power in bringing home to them the necessity of maintaining a high standard of order, patience and power of suspending judgment.

It has been said that in some respects Miss Clough presented a marked contrast to Dr. Sidgwick. This contrast may be partly described by saying that he saw things more in the abstract, she in the concrete. Not that he looked only at general principles and she at isolated instances (for both took large views without neglecting the single examples), but still the distinction was evident. Both had risen by a painful process of mental and moral self-culture above conventional views as to the world and man's place in it, but in Sidgwick the search was chiefly inspired by a passion for truth, in Miss Clough by a desire to promote individual happiness. She naturally referred questions to present cases. Thus—if certain subjects were said to be necessary as preliminaries to a University course, she would at once think whether A. or B. would be the better for having studied Latin or Mathematics. She allowed for diversity of all kinds among students and other persons with whom she had to do. A rule was important to her as touching actual cases, not the cases as exemplifying the rule. She was strong physically and indifferent to discomfort and hardship in all that she undertook. Yet she had no belief in asceticism, and exhorted her students to " take the little pleasures of life." It was her own idea to begin hockey at Newnham, then a most novel suggestion, which brought at first some ridicule and even disapprobation from select circles. She naturally understood and liked some of her students better than others—but even those who had less than others of her special intimacy were at times pleased and stimulated by finding how much of her goodwill they possessed and how she had plans for their future. If her character broadened and mellowed with years, it was not that she was ever intolerant or unsympathetic, but that she responded to the affection and respect of those who knew and appreciated her. She, too, had a sense of humour which enlivened the community from the beginning, and the respect with which both

her name and her character were held in the highest
University circles more than counteracted an
occasional innocent unconventionality in her social
intercourse.

It may seem almost invidious to choose some and
omit others among the earliest friends of Newnham,
in awarding due meed of praise and gratitude, but
certainly the two who have been lightly sketched
here were undoubtedly the foremost of Newnham's
benefactors. Early students will remember others
who have passed away : the Miss Kennedys, with
their kind and gracious hospitality, and care for
the rather homeless persons who ranked among
" out-students " ; Mr. Coutts Trotter, who was
Chairman of the Council, and left his library to the
College ; Mr. W. H. H. Hudson, who was financial
adviser and auditor for 33 years ; Mr. Archer-Hind,
who placed his refined scholarship at the disposal
of mere beginners in Greek, was always willing
to make one lesson swell out into two—and took
no fees ; Mr. Main, the standby of the earliest
students of Natural Science ; Mr. Marshall, who
created and directed an enthusiastic devotion to
the study of Economics ; Mrs. Bateson, who originally dispensed the lecture tickets to students entering
their course, and whose parties at St. John's Lodge
were highly appreciated ;—and many more.

The students who were first attracted to the
opportunities for women in Cambridge were, as a

rule, somewhat more mature, though less well instructed, than those of later times. There were exceptions in this latter respect, as in the case of the late Miss Edith Creak, well known in the educational world, who was the daughter of a schoolmaster, and who passed successfully both the mathematical and the classical triposes at the age of nineteen. Another of the original five was Mrs. Armitage (*née* Bulley), who has written much on early English antiquities and is an authority on Barrows. Among the first to take Triposes were Miss Paley (now Mrs. A. Marshall) and Miss Amy Bulley, who were successful in the Moral Sciences Tripos in 1874, Miss Mary Kennedy, afterwards Mrs. R. T. Wright, in the same Tripos in 1875, and Miss Felicia Larner who took the Historical Tripos in 1875. These ladies were all examined by private favour of the examiners, the greatest care being taken that all formalities should be duly observed. Only, they were admitted after passing certain Groups of the Women's Examinations instead of the Previous Examination, and, in one or two cases, were allowed a longer time of preparation than the University regulations prescribed.

The exaggerated dread of triposes and admiration for those who achieved them makes an amusing feature in early Newnham days. It would now seem absurd for a college to exult over second class honours. But every successful student helped to destroy some of the "hasty generalizations" repeated outside as to women in triposes, the first being that they would fail or else break down in health. When they succeeded and remained vigorous, it was said that they might get through but would not get first classes. When they obtained first classes in the newer triposes, it was declared that they would never get a first class in classics or mathematics. The death-blow to all these hypotheses came in 1890, when Miss Philippa Fawcett's name was read in the Senate House as "above the Senior Wrangler." There was a kind of poetic justice in this event, as Miss Fawcett's parents had been earnest and effectual helpers of the movement from the very beginning.

This, however, is to anticipate events. During the early days in Regent Street, good work was being done, and the students had a happy life, but they were cooped in a small space, and the friends of the movement had to seek both a larger home and more funds to sustain it. From 1872-1874, Miss Clough and the students found a congenial house of residence behind St. John's College. This was Merton Hall, an old manor house with a very pleasant garden and other attractions. Here something like collegiate life was first begun—with a debating society, games (with limitations) and various collective interests. Another house in Trumpington Street was hired to accommodate the

MERTON HALL, 1872-1874.

overflow of students. A few who had been attracted by the lectures, but for some reason were unable or unwilling to enter a hall of residence, formed a kind of outer circle. These " out-students " were made to feel less of outsiders by the kind and hospitable attention bestowed on them by Miss Marion Kennedy. Their number tended to diminish, as membership of a college or hall came to be desirable on social and disciplinary grounds. When the College was more definitely constituted, all who wished to become regular students were obliged to reside either in a Hall of Newnham or with parents and guardians, exceptions only being allowed in the case of women above the under-graduate age.[1]

Meantime arrangements were being made to secure a more permanent place of residence. To meet what had become a necessity, it was proposed to form a Company, which, after the choice of a site near the village of Newnham, was called the Newnham Hall Company. There was, however, a singular absence of commercial acquisitiveness or speculation in the Society which bore this financial designation. A good deal of the money subscribed came from benefactors who so far from seeking profit from their investments continued their gifts

---

[1] Here it may be noted that a different arrangement obtains at Oxford, where there is a Society of Home Students who are not attached to any College or Hall.

for many years. Mention may be made of Miss
Ewart, Mr. and Mrs. Stephen Winkworth, Miss
Bonham Carter among other munificent benefactors.[1]
A good many well-wishers who could not give
princely contributions were ready to make the
venture of faith and to subscribe for shares. The
result was that in 1875 Newnham Hall was opened
and Miss Clough with the students entered into
residence. They had during 1874-75 occupied a
dwelling in Bateman Street where Miss Clough had
ingeniously secured the use of a house-and-a-half
which she made into one. Newnham Hall was a
Queen Anne building, of red brick, which has
mellowed after its forty years. The architect, Mr.
Basil Champneys, took a strong personal interest
in its original plan and subsequent extension.
Those who knew it when it was simply Newnham
Hall (later called the *South*, now the *Old Hall*) must
feel a little regret that its imposing south front—
intended to be the actual front—is only seen by a
minority of casual visitors. In fact, no one knew
in '75 in what direction, if in any, it might have to
expand, and there is a story current that in the
plans, the possibility was considered of transforming
it—if a hall for women students proved a failure—
into two ordinary dwelling-houses.

The College, formally so-called, came into existence
by the amalgamation of the two societies, " The

---

[1] A list of Benefactors is in preparation.

Association for the promotion of the Higher Education of Women in Cambridge " (more briefly called the
" Lectures Association ") and the " Newnham Hall
Company, Limited," in 1880. The new title adopted
was " The Newnham College Association for advancing Education and Learning among Women in
Cambridge." Before this time, the " College "
only existed in idea, but that existence, as we have
seen, was a very real one. Even when it attained
its first permanent habitation, it was—for a college
—small, as in 1876 there were only about thirty
students besides the out-students. But it had a
respectable, academic-looking exterior, and life within
was vigorous. Among the residents was Miss Paley,
now Mrs. Marshall, whom the students with pride
regarded as their earliest don, one of the first five,
and one of the earliest to take a tripos. She proved
a very successful teacher of Political Economy, a
popular subject among the early students, many of
whom were ambitious of some career of social
activity. Classical students were few, but very
eager. Miss J. E. Harrison and Miss K. Corfe took
their tripos in 1879. Natural Sciences were pursued
with ardour and success, partly through the liberality
of St. John's College in admitting Newnham students
to their laboratory before the Newnham laboratory
was built. The first student to obtain a first class
was Miss Ogle, afterwards Mrs. Koppel, in 1876.
It is gratifying that her daughter afterwards became

a Newnham student, and has made herself educa-
tionally useful in South Africa. Mathematics held
its own. The Historical Tripos, when separated
from the Law, attracted several students. Those
who took Moral Sciences, as already said, enjoyed
the special attention of Mr. Sidgwick.

These candidates were all, of course, examined
informally, *i.e.* by special favour of individual
examiners. It was from the first desired by Mr.
Sidgwick that any student who showed, by marked
success in the Women's Examination or in any
other way, that she had real aptitude for intellectual
culture, should be encouraged to proceed to a
Tripos. But in the early days the Tripos students
were not the only ones who were capable of good
intellectual work. Some, as has been said, for
one reason or another, did not follow the lines
then laid down for Triposes, and the variety was—
socially and intellectually—an excellent thing for
the students. Specialization in study is often
bound to have a narrowing effect. But by student
friendships, young people learn to care for things
in heaven and earth that will never lie within their
special province. It is a good thing for Cambridge,
and consequently for Newnham, that there is no such
iron bar fixed there between Sciences and Arts,
as often, in other educational institutions, tends
to prejudice and narrowness. There may be, before
definite lines are fixed, tendencies to too much

diffusion ; this, however, was prevented by the general system of tuition.

As yet, in 1879, there were not many resident tutors to settle the work of students in their several departments. But competent University men were always ready to put their knowledge and experience at the service of a student choosing her University course. Indeed the helpfulness of men on whom the students had no claim, is one of the brightest features, even of the bright days of Newnham's beginnings.

Newnham Hall had from the first a fairly large garden, not very minutely laid out,[1] but large enough for tennis, for which game an ash court was made. A gymnasium, in the pre-games period, seemed a necessity, and was erected and opened in 1877. Before that time, students had been allowed to go at stated times to the gymnasium in the town, and strange now to relate, some did so with great enthusiasm. But the interest in indoor gymnastics declined with the greater facility for out-door sport, of which more later on.

Newnham Hall was more in the country then than the College is at present. It must be remembered that married dons with their families were a comparatively new institution, the residential

---

[1] The present writer enjoyed one evening the privilege of being deputed, with some other students, by Miss Clough, to drive out some cows who had strayed into the garden.

quarter to the west did not exist at this time in Cambridge, and certainly Newnham was in the pleasantest part of Cambridge for country walks. " Constitutionals " are now out of favour, but the early students enjoyed the " Grantchester Grind," —especially when the marsh-marigolds were out, and the Madingley Woods with their blue-bells, and the Roman Road in blue flax season ; and the Backs were very near; there were nightingales too whose nocturnal songs were by some found almost too penetrating.   There was an atmosphere, in town and country, favourable to cheerfulness, to the formation of friendships, to the development of intellectual and social activity, to the enlargement of opportunities for women in forwarding the betterment of the world.   It was a time of hope for youth, seen not only in the pioneer students, but in those champions of their cause, some themselves young, some older, whose efforts for the next generation were ever strenuous and cheerful, none the less so for the experience of resistance from old-world inertia and the dead weight of prejudice which only patience and wisdom could ever prevail to lift.

CHAPTER II

NEWNHAM COLLEGE IN ADOLESCENCE

THE early part of the eighties was full of events for the women students of Newnham and their supporters. In these years they obtained (1) a fixed legal constitution ; (2) a second hall of residence, and other much needed buildings ; (3) gradual increase of facilities for study, especially in the opening of Cambridge College lectures to women ; (4) more important still, a large measure of University recognition, and (5) greater opportunities of educational and social work for past students. These several lines of progress may here be taken in order, except the fifth, which I reserve for the next chapter.

(1) It has been mentioned that when the necessity arose of increasing accommodation for women students, an amalgamation was in 1879 discussed of the *Association for the Higher Education of Women in Cambridge* with the *Newnham Hall Company*. The Memorandum and Articles of Association were drawn up before long, and Newnham College came

c   33

into existence and was registered in the spring of
1880. The constitution was not entirely according
to the character of an Academic institution, being
under the financial control of the Board of Trade.
There was a provision that no profits should
accrue to members of the College in the legal
sense of the word *members*, though members
might receive remuneration for work done for
the College. The Ordinary Members consisted of
the first promoters of the College, with large sub-
scribers to its funds afterwards ; Associate Members
(helpers and benefactors, not to be confounded with
the present Associates) ; and Honorary Members,
mostly teachers and helpers of the students. The
government rested with a Council, to be elected at
a general meeting of Members of the College, four
going out annually in rotation, but re-eligible. The
executive officers were to be a President, Vice-
President, and Secretary. The President and the
Principal were to be *ex officio* members. There
was as yet no systematic representation of quasi-
graduate students, but the resident lecturers were
as a rule entitled to vote as ordinary or as honorary
members.

We shall see later on in what respects this Memorandum of Association came to be regarded as
inadequate. In point of fact, it marked progress
in stability, and worked very well for many
years. The Council generally consisted of persons

enthusiastically devoted to the interests of the College, and many of them able, by their experience on educational bodies or by their social influence, to assist in its development along the best lines.

(2) Materially, the great event of 1880-81 was the completion and opening of the second Hall of Residence, the North Hall, as it was called, the name South Hall being given to the earlier Newnham Hall. The ground on which it was built was on the other side of a narrow road. In the day-time, when gates could be kept open, passage from one Hall to the other was easy, but at night, for privacy's sake, it was necessary that they should be closed. This, of course, was a check to late evening parties for cocoa, chat, or dancing, among the students belonging to separate Halls, and the concession of one open evening a week hardly met the difficulty. There seemed to be a danger lest *Hall* feeling might endanger devotion to the College as a whole, and one might expect that the fact of the Principal residing in the older building and only a Vice-Principal in the newer might seem to imply some kind of inferiority. Any danger of the kind was avoided by an act of generous devotion on the part of two promoters of the College which could hardly have been foretold.

The great services of Dr. Sidgwick to the incipient College have been alluded to, though they are far

too wide and various to be severally recorded.[1]
His wife, formerly Miss Eleanor Balfour, had for
some years been a very able treasurer and member of
council. She had given a scholarship to Newnham
in Mathematics, her own chief subject of study at
that time. They lived a quiet, scholarly, but
sociable life in their house at Hillside, at the beginning
of the Chesterton Road. At this moment, when
anyone of less standing in the University and the
world generally could hardly have met the emer-
gency, Mrs. Sidgwick agreed to come and preside
in the new Hall, with the title of Vice-Principal,
and Mr. Sidgwick came to live there also, thus
giving up his privacy and the company of most of
his books. The arrangement was the more successful
in that Miss Gladstone also took up residence in the
North Hall as her secretary. The name of Gladstone
brought distinction with it. Miss Helen Gladstone
had resided as a student of English and Political
Economy for one year with the Sidgwicks and for
two years in Newnham Hall, and was deservedly
popular both with the students and in the University
world outside. Students who entered the College,

---

[1] Including financial help. Miss B. A. Clough (in the life of
A. J. C.) mentions how when treasurer, Mr. Sidgwick used to
fail to present the coal and gas bills. There was a legend in
Newnham Hall that once when Miss Clough wanted a new
frying-pan, she had to apply to Mr. Sidgwick for the money.
On one occasion when furnishing the house in Regent Street, he
gave up a continental holiday for the sake of the cause.

and were taken into the new Hall, cherished ever after the memory of these two years as a halcyon time—in which they enjoyed listening to good talk and associating with interesting persons more than during any other period of their lives. At the end of two years, Miss Gladstone became Vice-Principal, resident in the North Hall, a post which she held for many years, and in which her well-known geniality, cheerfulness, and whole-hearted devotion to her task and to the students under her care found abundant scope and recognition.

It was under the same roof as the North Hall that the much needed lecture rooms were raised.   There were at first three.   Later when a large number of small rooms for private teaching were made in the Pfeiffer Building, two of the lecture rooms proper were knocked into one, thereby giving the College one room large enough to accommodate (if desks were removed) about a hundred people. It was chiefly by pressure from Miss Gladstone that an infirmary or hospital was built, adjoining the North Hall, but with its separate entrance. This has often proved useful in checking the spread of infectious ailments among the students or the servants. A chemical laboratory had already been erected in the garden at a respectful distance from the original Hall. Its equipment was mainly the task of Miss Penelope Lawrence, afterwards head-mistress of Roedean School, Brighton. A laboratory for the study of Biological subjects was provided in the town in 1884, a disused Congregational chapel being adapted to the purpose. Mrs. Sidgwick and her sister, Miss Alice Balfour, were the principal donors, and the laboratory was appropriately named after their brother, Francis Maitland Balfour, whose promising and already distinguished career had been cut short by an accident in the Alps. For many years, these two laboratories formed the training ground of a large number of students, who did much to supply the demand for improved science teaching in schools and colleges for girls. In the Chemical Laboratory Miss Freund and in the Balfour Laboratory Miss Greenwood (now Mrs. Bidder) and Miss Saunders presided for many years, carrying on both teaching and research. (Both Miss Freund and Mrs. Bidder were former students of Girton.) In course of time, the opening of the University laboratories to women students rendered these buildings less necessary, and they are at present let for University purposes.

With the increase in the number of students, further buildings became necessary. The South Hall (formerly Newnham Hall) had been designed with a view to possible extension, and in 1882, a west wing was built, containing rooms for about twelve more students. The ground floor of this building was devoted to a well-planned Library, at that time a great desideratum. The equipment of the

College as to books had originally been scanty.
Perhaps the need of books was, for a time, not
altogether to be deplored, as the early generation
of students realized the necessity of procuring their
own books or of inducing generous friends to assist
them in that direction ; and many gave books as
a parting present to the College.   A moderate-sized
common-room in the Old Hall (since divided into
two rooms for students) was the first library, but
was soon outgrown.   But when something larger
was required, the new Library (now the Reading
Room of the Old Hall) both served its purpose till
the books again outran the accommodation, and
afforded a delightful morning room for study, as
well as space for occasional social parties.

(3) During the late 'seventies and the early
'eighties, women students were informally admitted
to privileges which greatly facilitated their work,
and in particular many College lectures were opened
to them.   Their own lectures—before the building
of Sidgwick Hall—were given in the rooms belonging
to the Young Men's Christian Association, near the
old Post Office, a central but somewhat noisy situation.   The larger rooms in this building were of
good size and convenient, but the class-rooms were
less so, and to many students their first introduction
to Greek Tragedy or to English Law will always be
associated with the striking of a hammer on the
blacksmith's anvil.   The new lecture rooms at

Newnham had not this drawback. The professorial
lectures were generally given in rooms now absorbed
in the University Library. In some, women were
allowed to come into the gallery, where their presence was not easily discerned. But meantime, as
already mentioned, some of the Colleges were ready
to accept suggestions as to admitting women to the
Inter-collegiate Lectures. The first of the Colleges
to admit women to lectures in its own hall was
Christ's. In the summer term of 1876, eight
students of Newnham College (some working at
classics, others at history) were admitted to a
course of lectures on the Punic Wars given by
Mr. (now Professor) J. S. Reid in the temporary
dining-hall of Christ's. Great efforts were made to
meet the somewhat exacting demands—in those
days—of social propriety. Thus these students
were obliged always to be chaperoned by a responsible lady, and as Miss Clough had in the early days
few colleagues to lighten her responsibilities, the
task usually fell on her. Needless to say, she never
represented this as a grievance, though the lectures
were three times a week, the hour inconvenient, and
the weather generally wet. She was only too glad
to help in a new departure, and, as she said (with
reminiscences of her brother and Dr. Arnold), she
always found Roman History interesting.

King's was the next College to admit women.
Trinity not till a little later. It may be noticed,

without any disparagement of the lecturers who obtained these concessions, that in the case of those already lecturing to women according to the previous arrangements, it was more convenient to have seats assigned to the women in the College lecture rooms or halls than to give the same lecture to their men pupils in College in the morning and to the women in a room belonging to the Young Men's Christian Association, or even in Newnham College, in the afternoon. Nevertheless Newnham owes gratitude to the Lecturers and to the Fellows of Colleges who showed, in many cases, both zeal and courtesy in meeting the women students' needs. With regard to the undergraduates, it may be remarked that though at first some showed a curious amazement mixed with bashfulness at their strange visitors, they soon accustomed themselves to the change, and showed almost always a spirit of courtesy and good sense. As more accommodation came to be provided by the University—irrespective of College distinctions—in the New Divinity Schools and the New Lecture Rooms, access to lectures became easier for women, as for other non-members of the University.

Another great advantage which the students obtained in these years was permission to read in the University Library. They could not be admitted without referees, such as were demanded from non-university persons, but the Principal was always accepted as one referee, so that the student candidate had to find one only. Fees—very moderate—were paid by the College when a student had been specially advised to read in the Library. Formal admission was granted for the morning only, but a student who for any special reason wished to read in the afternoon as well could easily obtain permission.

Another privilege gradually obtained without any special effort was that of being examined in the Inter-collegiate Examinations popularly called *Mays*. As all Cambridge men and women know, examinations of students in their first and second years are held in most subjects at the end of the summer term, to test their knowledge and power of expressing it.   These are not directly under any University board, but are given by the lecturers on the subjects they have been teaching, in various Colleges, during the past year.   The " Mays," in spite of drawbacks, have often been of great value, in giving confidence to industrious but despondent students, and in warning those whose progress was unsatisfactory. The fact of having been through a certain course, examined on the subject, and marked with the undergraduates, emphasised the fact to the women students, the undergraduates, and the world at large, that the work done at Newnham and Girton was really of University standing.

(4) All these steps led towards what was necessary

in order that the work of the College should be solid and permanent—the recognition by the University of the existence of women students and women of what I have called quasi-graduate status. It may be said—it was said, and still is said when further demands are made—that women had the real thing, why trouble about the artificial trappings ? Women could become well-educated, even learned ; those who had studied at Cambridge were the better esteemed in educational circles, and they were free from many tiresome responsibilities that weigh on full members of the University. But to this was answered : that the path to good education and sound learning is still more thorny than it need be ; that the world, which often has to distribute educational posts and distinctions, does not care for education without a degree ; that the position of the women, held only by courtesy, was insecure. A scrupulous examiner might at any time decline to examine a tripos-candidate whom he was not bound to examine, and any University lecturer might refuse to allow women at his lectures. At the same time, women who " brushed the flounce of all the sciences," and flitted about like bees for intellectual honey, might easily pose as University women and bring real students into disrepute. Finally : if there *were* duties as well as privileges exacted from the children of Alma Mater, women would hardly be found unwilling to accept them.

Matters came to a crisis at the end of the year 1880. In the winter 1879-1880 (the triposes came, then, at various periods of the year), Newnham and Girton obtained first classes in three triposes, the most conspicuous case being that of Miss C. A. Scott of Girton, who in the Mathematical Tripos had obtained (by the usual informal examination) a place equal to that of the eighth wrangler. These successes seemed to give a *reductio ad absurdum* to the common arguments about the inferiority of the " female mind," to set the mark of success on the methods followed at both Colleges, and to suggest the inexpediency—if not injustice—of withholding from women the title which should give them status and improve their prospects in the academic world. It may be mentioned that, in 1878, London University had obtained a supplement to its Charter empowering it to admit women to its degrees, a step which marked both a recognition of the claims of educated women and an abandonment of London's first tentative measures in providing examinations for women. It had for some time admitted women to a " General Examination," closely resembling the Matriculation, but allowing more option as to subjects. This might be followed by examinations for certificates of Higher Proficiency, which could be taken, without further fee, with the General, or in any subsequent year. It was a very useful examination for girls who had left school and in continuing their studies at home wished to take up one subject or another, together or at intervals, according to convenience. The weak points were that the syllabus did not sufficiently correspond to the men's to give any guarantee as to standard demanded and attained—and far worse : that there was nothing progressive about the " Special " examinations, there being only one examination held in each subject. When the degree examinations were thrown open, a good many Cambridge women took the London B.A. or M.A. *after* their triposes in order to have some title to present to the academic world. But—as London degrees examinations were then arranged—such work generally involved the consumption of much time on other than specially chosen lines on the part of any Cambridge Tripos student. The fact that it was desired and achieved gave proof—if fresh proof were needed—of the actual market value to educated women of the letters denoting a certain standard of mental equipment. London University was then, it may be added, a University only in name. The teaching tested in its examinations had been obtained by solitary students reading privately, by residents in various provincial Colleges, and by members of those Colleges in London—University, King's, Bedford, and Westfield, which were ready to take their place as Colleges of an actual teaching as well as degree-granting University—as London became in

1900. The provincial Universities (Manchester, Birmingham, Bristol, etc.) all admitted women to their degrees early, if not at their first opening.

But to return to Cambridge. The movement of 1880 was taken up in various quarters, notably in the North of England. Petitions were drawn up and sent to the Senate of the University praying for degrees for women. That originated by Mr. and Mrs. Aldis of Newcastle declared : " That the present plan of informal examination is unsatisfactory, and that consequently the undersigned persons interested in the Higher Education of Women pray the Senate of the University to give women the right of admission to the degree examination and to degrees." Three other memorials were presented. The Executive Committee of Girton College, after pointing to the satisfactory results of several years' experience, desired the University to " take their case (that of the Students) into serious consideration, with a view to their formal admission to the B.A. degree." This was, of course, different from the Newcastle petition in being of the nature of a compromise, since it did not ask for the M.A. which would have involved a share in the government of the University. A similar half-way measure had previously been adopted with regard to Nonconformists, to whom the B.A. had been allowed some time before they were admitted to the M.A.

The third petition is that which specially interests us in the history of Newnham College, as it was that of the Lectures Committee, out of which—as already related—Newnham College took its beginning. This document, like that of Girton, appeals to the result of experience, though not to experience of exactly the same kind. It expresses a desire that a stable form may be given to the plan of instruction and examination already being carried on, and also a preference that some option should be allowed as to the Previous Examination ; and unwillingness (not refusal) to prepare women for the Ordinary Degree.

A fourth memorial, much to the same general purpose as the last, was signed by a hundred and twenty-three members of the University.

The result of the Memorials was that a Syndicate was appointed, a memorable discussion on its proposals held in the Art Schools, and the " Graces " drawn up to be submitted to the whole Senate. Among the staunchest supporters of the proposals were the venerable, whole-hearted helper of the cause, Prof. Benjamin Hall Kennedy, Dr. (later Bishop) Browne, Prof. Cayley, Dr. (now Prof.) H. Jackson, Prof. J. E. B. Mayor, Dr. Peile, and Mr. Coutts Trotter. These name sufficiently refute any accusation of youthful flightiness or over-strained liberalism in the character of the movement.

As the *Graces* have formed from that time the basis of Newnham College as an institution sanctioned by the University, and as their purport is not always clearly apprehended, it may be as well to transcribe them in full, excepting only such as relate to financial and subordinate regulations :

1. Female students who have fulfilled the conditions respecting length of residence and standing which Members of the University are required to fulfil may be admitted to the Previous Examination, and the Tripos Examinations.

2. Such residence shall be kept (*a*) at Girton College or (*b*) at Newnham College, or (*c*) within the precincts of the University under the regulations of one or other of these Colleges, or (*d*) in any similar Institution within the precincts of the University, which may be recognised hereafter by the University by Grace of the Senate.

3. Certificates of residence shall be given by the authorities of Girton College or Newnham College or other similar institution hereafter recognised by the University in the same form as that which is customary in the case of Members of the University.

4. Except as provided in Regulation 5, female students shall before admission to a Tripos Examination have passed the Previous Examination (including the Additional Subjects) or one of the examinations which excuse Members of the University from the Previous Examination.

5. Female students who have obtained an Honour Certificate in the Higher Local Examination may be admitted to a Tripos Examination, though such certificate does not cover the special portions of the Higher Local Examinations which are accepted by the University in lieu of parts or the whole of the Previous Examination ; provided that such students have passed in Group B (Languages) and Group C (Mathematics).

6. No female student shall be admitted to any part of any of the Examinations of the University who is not recommended for admission by the authorities of the College or other institution to which she has been admitted.

7. After each examination, a Class List of the female students who have satisfied the Examiners shall be published by the Examiners at the same time with the Class List of Members of the University, the standard for each Class and the method of arrangement in each Class being the same in the two Class Lists.

8. In each class of female students in which the names are arranged in order of merit, the place which each of such students would have occupied in the corresponding Class of Members of the University shall be indicated.

9. The Examiners for a Tripos shall be at liberty to state, if the case be so, that a female candidate shall have failed to satisfy them or has in their

opinion reached a standard equivalent to that required from Members of the University for the Ordinary B.A. degree.

10. To each female student who has satisfied the Examiners in a Tripos Examination, a Certificate shall be given by the University stating the conditions under which she was admitted to the examinations of the University, the Examinations in which she has satisfied the Examiner, and the Class and place in the Class, if indicated, to which she has attained, in each of such examinations.

It was further provided that these arrangements should hold, in the first instance, for five years. Rules were laid down as to the conditions under which any future Hall of residence might be recognised by the admission of its students to Triposes.

The result of the voting on the Graces was looked forward to by both sides with hope and fear. The result was a triumphant majority for the women's cause, 331 to 32. The small number who actually voted against the Graces does not, of course, imply that the number of objectors was insignificant, for, in fact, a good many opponents withdrew early as from a lost cause. From that time, Feb. 24th, 1881, counted as the great day of the College to be remembered by all succeeding generations of students, who have been annually reminded at Commemoration how well their friends had fought for them, how a special train had been run from

London to accommodate favourable members of Parliament, and with what joy and thankfulness the news had been received in the College and telegraphed to friends at a distance.

The cause for congratulation was very real. If things had gone otherwise, it is difficult to see what the future of women's education in England would have been. Oxford was temporarily behind Cambridge in the movement, and a set-back at Cambridge would certainly have damaged prospects in the sister University, and, in fact, throughout England. Women would have been debarred from sharing in the best that University education in England can give, and would have been cut off from the historic sources of sound learning and of moral and intellectual inspiration.

A perusal of the Graces will show that though they gave all that was immediately needed, they did not satisfy all the actual or possible desires of the promoters of women's colleges. Outsiders, as before mentioned, already wished for full membership to be granted. To many this seemed a premature project. Yet those were right who foresaw that a desire for more complete membership was certain to come by and by. In 1881 there were few, if any, of the women quasi-graduates able to take an active part in University work. Some apprenticeship, under the wing of Alma Mater, might seem at least desirable. Again, the views held by Girton, that conditions of examinations such as those relating to preliminary qualifications and the Pass degree, ought from the first to have been the same for women as for members of the University, might be urged with some force. As already shown, the objection to compulsory Classics and Mathematics, even up to the standard of the Previous Examination, on the part of some of the founders and supporters of Newnham College was due, not to a preference for easier conditions, but from a fear of a detrimental effect on schools. In point of fact, so many other alternatives than those of the Previous Examination and the Higher Local are now offered that neither of these examinations is much favoured in the best schools that send girls up to the Universities. As to the Pass Degree : the suspicion with which it was regarded by the Newnham pioneers has already been noticed. The objection to it is not that it is bad in itself : many attempts have been made to render a pass course interesting and profitable to men who have not physical strength or intellectual persistency to embark on an honours curriculum, or who wish to reduce their academic duties in order to follow some social or intellectual hobbies. But there has always been the danger of demanding a very small amount of intellectual work and tolerating men who have no leaning towards academic pursuits, and to whom the University is chiefly attractive by reason of its scope for athletics and for genial life in comradeship. There was as yet, and it is to be hoped there will be permanently, no place in the women's colleges for the society woman without intellectual aspirations. Such an element would have been difficult to deal with, and would not have been successful from any point of view. True, Newnham never wished to discourage either students of discursive mind and original ideas and plans, or those who—through defective early education or delicate health—shrunk from a tripos course. In fact, some students whose presence and work in the College have proved eminently beneficial to themselves and to Newnham, have preferred to take a mixed course of study. For the rank and file, it is now supposed that the numerous triposes afford sufficient choice. If, at the end of her second year, a student is judged to be unable to proceed further on tripos lines, she is expected to go down, unless her studies are judged to be sufficiently serious and profitable for giving special leave to continue them. The equivalent of a pass degree is, as already stated, and as set forth in No. 9 of the Graces, only awarded to a student who has narrowly escaped failure. It may also be noticed that a failure, for a woman, leaves no chance of a second trial.

The Graces gave a real and substantial benefit to women students and—indirectly—to those who had

been, informally, through a tripos course at Newnham. These latter did not obtain University
recognition of any sort, but their names and tripos
places were recorded in the Girton and Newnham
Calendars, and this served as evidence of their
standing to the educational world. When Trinity
College, Dublin, for a few years (as will be hereafter related) granted an *ad eundem* B.A. or M.A.
to Oxford and Cambridge women who had taken
final honours examinations, those who had done so
previous to the Graces (as will be hereafter noticed) [1]
were admitted with the others. For some reason,
those who many years later drew up the Representation of the People Act of 1918 felt obliged
to draw the line more strictly and to limit the vote
to those women who had obtained the equivalent
of a degree since 1881.

There were no heart-burnings caused by the comparatively narrow range of the privileges given by
the Graces, partly because it was always felt that
more would come quietly as time and occasion should
dictate. The resident staff, as such, obtained no
recognition. No woman could sit on a board of
studies, nor lecture formally in an academic building. Privately, the opinion of Newnham lecturers
was sometimes asked on a question as to curricula,
and women of distinction occasionally lectured and
sometimes drew large audiences, while—in course

[1] See page 110 seq.

of time—some undergraduates were advised by their tutors to seek admission to the lectures of a Newnham specialist. For some years there was no ground for formal extensions of privilege. And it was believed, and was to be proved again afterwards, that in the situation in which Newnham found itself, it was unwise to demand privileges that were not almost certain to be granted.

In fact, the crowning triumph of the Graces marks the success of the policy of Miss Clough, Dr. and Mrs. Sidgwick, Miss Kennedy, and the other founders of the College : a policy of winning great things by not standing out for lesser ones, of pertinacity in following a large if at first vague programme, and of conciliation and " sweet reasonableness " towards those who looked askance on the whole movement. It must be observed that all the Founders were deeply imbued with love and reverence for the University, and that the students were brought up to regard it as almost an Alma Mater—at any rate, as a noble and worthy corporation, to which they owed a deep debt for its past doings, and for what it had always stood for in the nation and in the world, a debt increased by the privilege granted to them of living within its precincts and learning wisdom from its most distinguished sons. There was no " battering at the gates." The pioneers of the Women's Colleges, so far from tolerating any notion that the University would suffer from granting their requests, would have felt it a thing worth much labour and many struggles if they could in any way add to the great repute and dignity which Cambridge had, among Universities, enjoyed from far-back times.

CHAPTER III

NEWNHAM COLLEGE IN PROGRESS

THE time between the recognition of Newnham
College by the University of Cambridge, in 1881,
and the deeply mourned death of its chief founder
and first Principal, in February 1892, is one of
expansion and progress, both as regards the actual
College buildings and the various activities of past
and present students, especially in educational and
social work.

The building of the North Hall has been mentioned, and also the increase in size of the South
Hall, with the building of a library, not adequate
to the subsequent needs of the College, but sufficient for the number of students then in residence,
and afterwards very useful as a reading room and
a supplementary library for duplicate books. In
1885 a fives court was erected on the north side of
the College buildings. Meantime, a third Hall was
projected, and, owing to the munificence of various
benefactors, constructed on a liberal scale, and was
ready for opening in 1888. It may be mentioned

that one benefactor, Mr. Stephen Winkworth, earned
the gratitude of subsequent students by granting a
special sum to provide for the building of students'
rooms of somewhat larger dimensions than the
smaller ones in the other two Halls.   Mr. and Mrs.
Winkworth, old friends of Miss Clough, had taken
interest in Newnham from the beginning, and their
only daughter had been a student there.

As we are thus brought to the consideration of
students' rooms, I might mention a line of progress
initiated by the students themselves, and afterwards followed up by the authorities.   In early
days a separate study for each student had not
been contemplated.   This is another difference
between Newnham and Girton, since, in the latter
College, the collegiate idea had been more prominent
from the first, and each Girton student had her
bedroom and sitting-room, however small.   In the
first abode of Miss Clough and her five students
all slept in *bona fide* bedrooms and worked sitting
round a common table.   In the early Newnham
Hall more arrangement was made for privacy in
study.   Each student had her little writing table
and sufficient book-shelves in her room.   But the
common sitting-rooms were used for most of the
day, and not many rooms occupied by individual
students were suitable for receiving company.
Even little tea-parties among the students were of
a very picnicky character.   But when the ambition

of the students was set on making a study-bedroom into a study first and a bedroom in a very secondary place, ingenuity provided facilities. Although the matter may seem *infiniment petit*, I consider that among Newnham pioneers the two students who accomplished this revolution should hold a place. One of them bought a large piece of chintz, and undisturbed by the jests of some of her comrades and the amused criticism of Miss Clough, devised a covering for bedstead, chest of drawers and other pieces of bedroom furniture. The other, of more definitely artistic taste (it was in the days of "Patience" and of the so-called *aesthetic* movement for soft colours and flowing lines) procured a piece of sage-green cloth or cretonne, and effected a similar revolution. Already in the large corner rooms something like a cubicle arrangement had been devised. The evident preference of the students for harmoniously, if simply, furnished rooms and for the preponderance of the idea of study over that of mere rest was followed out in furnishing new rooms as they were required. Old oak hutches, bureaux, the drawers of which might hold clothes, bed-coverings of a character suitable to that of the room, also pretty wall-papers of the kind Morris had lately invented, were procured for the students generally. Thus students came to take more pleasure in their rooms, into which they could invite one another, and sometimes friends from outside, though the common sitting-rooms were still the usual place for receiving guests. I think I am not wrong in saying that Newnham here started a practice subsequently followed in almost all houses of residence for women students. Certainly the first head of Somerville, when visiting Miss Clough, showed interest in the study-bedroom system. The desire to make the one room assert its diurnal rather than its nocturnal character was not new. Dickens had already ridiculed it in describing the " rooms " of Dick Swiveller. But the solution of the problem on principles of both convenience and beauty was, perhaps, first found in Newnham Hall during the early days.

I would pass to another—far more important— subject touching the relation of the students to the building in which they resided : it has puzzled some people how it has come about that with all the building, a chapel has never formed part of Newnham College. The subject is a delicate one, and I only take it up here because of the very erroneous and sometimes damaging explanations that have been assigned for the omission. Worst of all to those familiar with the leaders of the move- ment is the supposition that to them religion was a matter of indifference. For those who really knew Miss Clough, and others whom, while they still live, it seems indecent to mention—any such accusation is not only false but absurd. Miss

Clough's religion was one that illuminated all her work and gave her strength and patience to carry it on. She was, besides, sincerely attached to the Church of England. At the same time, having lived in America, and mixed with persons of very varied religious opinions, she had early become very widely tolerant of the manifold ways in which a religious spirit manifests itself in different circles and different types of character. She had also seen the bad results of any attempt to force young people into religious observances which had become for them unmeaning or distasteful. Again : she had known vicariously, if not personally, the ferment of the Tractarian movement at Oxford, and the wave of scepticism that seemed to follow or even to accompany it. Also any disposition in her to avoid whatever might suggest the taking up of a distinctly denominational or even inter-denominational attitude in the government of the College was strengthened by the distinctly anti-sectarian principles of vigorous and powerful supporters. Possibly at that time, more than at the present, any definite recognition of religion or provision of religious services seemed impossible apart from some denominational bias. The well-meant attempt of one founder of another women's college to provide chapel services on undenominational lines had foundered on the quicksands of theological controversy, and well-nigh wrecked the College—till it was saved by the singular tact and sympathetic insight of its new Principal. When Miss Clough first came to Cambridge, she began, as we have seen, not with a College, but with a moderate-sized household, and her arrangements were those of an ordinary Christian house, including family prayers. There was no need in Cambridge, as in a country district, to provide Sunday services. A rule was laid down, at first, that students were expected to inform the Principal of the place of worship they chose to attend, but this proviso was intended rather to give the Principal the right to make such inquiry than to impose any restrictions on the students. Miss Clough always regarded religious teaching and observance as belonging to the family rather than to any educational establishment, and she thought it essential to allow students to keep up their ties with any church to which they or their parents might belong.

In some ways the absence of a religious centre to the College may have been a disadvantage, but if so, the fault was rather in the times than in any persons. In point of fact, there has never been wanting a strong religious element in Newnham life. At the same time the atmosphere has been favourable to interchange of religious ideas among persons of various types and experiences. No student was made unpopular by her religious views unless she asserted them in an aggressive way.

Most religious movements in Cambridge (and there have been many) since the beginnings of the College have made their influence felt within its precincts, and a large number of past students have devoted their lives to distinctly religious work, especially in distant lands, and such always look to the staff and students of their College for sympathy and encouragement.

This digression seemed necessary to correct prevalent misconceptions. To return to the general growth of the College in the eighties : attached to the new Hall of residence as its dining-hall was a beautiful College Hall, much larger than either of the other dining-rooms, and suggestions were made that the Staff with the students in all three Halls should dine together. This arrangement was, however, not easily compatible with the plan of division for tutorial purposes into three Halls. One desirable addition was a well-equipped kitchen. For a time the two Halls on the north side were supplied from the new kitchen ; but much later, when the new Hall to the west, Peile Hall, was built, a large central kitchen was constructed, and all four Halls were provided from it, the food being wheeled to each in covered trolleys and received on hot tables in the several Halls.

The opening of Clough Hall, as the new and largest Hall was named, was a great occasion for Newnham. It was a pleasant summer day (June

9th, 1888), and many friends came from a distance.
On the same day a degree was to be granted to
the son of the Prince of Wales (Prince Albert Victor),
and the Prince of Wales (Edward VII.) with the
Princess and the three young Princesses paid a
visit to the College. The students welcomed them
with song in the new dining-hall, a ballot having
first been taken among them as to who were the
best representative students to present bouquets.
This is probably the first and last occasion on
which, in Newnham, a critical decision had to be
made as to beauty, physical vigour and becoming
dress. The royal party walked across the garden
from the new Hall to the Principal's own rooms.
Next followed a delightful ceremony which be-
tokened both the respect and affection felt for one
of the most assiduous helpers of the College and
the beginnings of a new vista for Newnham in the
endowment of Research—the presentation to Miss
Marion Kennedy of a sum, which her friends had
raised, to found a Studentship bearing her name,
as an endowment for post-graduate work. There
had been since 1882, by the generosity of the Hon.
Selina Bathurst, a fund for encouraging advanced
work in Natural Science, and it seemed eminently
fitting that the possibility of promoting learning of
any kind should be associated with the revered
name of Kennedy. But perhaps the most moving
event of that day was almost unpremeditated.

The old students who had come from a distance, with those in residence, had a social supper in the large new Hall, after which Miss Clough, overcoming the reticence with which she habitually covered her deepest feelings, allowed all present to see more of her ideals and hopes, with her trust in their realization, than some of them had as yet known to be part of her character.

The new buildings necessitated a new nomenclature. The points of the compass were rejected in favour of the names of the founders. North Hall, which had been inaugurated by Mrs. Sidgwick's Vice-Principalship, became Sidgwick Hall, the new Hall was named Clough Hall, the South Hall—not being connected with any founder so intimately as with Miss Clough herself—retained a portion of its prestige in the title of the Old Hall. Other names of founders and benefactors were reserved for later additions to the College. Miss Clough herself took up residence in the Hall which bore her name. Miss Gladstone was still Vice-Principal in Sidgwick Hall ; Miss Jane Lee, a very earnest scholar of Italian literature, entirely devoted to the best interests of the College, became head of the Old Hall, also with the title of Vice-Principal. This title for the person presiding over one particular Hall, and giving special attention to the needs of the students in that Hall, became somewhat misleading, and has since been replaced by

E

that of Tutor, to which (in the Cambridge Colleges) it roughly corresponds. The Vice-Principal in each Hall had much more to do with house-keeping arrangements than later on, when more unity in this respect had been achieved and a regular Steward appointed. The Vice-Principals presided at table in their several Halls, corresponded with the parents of students, arranged, within the limits of a few simple laws, rules for the discipline of the students, read prayers in the morning; in fact, were generally responsible for the social, physical and moral requirements of the students. As, when there were only two Halls, Miss Gladstone held the office in Sidgwick Hall for many years, she imparted to it a certain character, and for a long time *the* V.-P. was a title regarded as almost individual to her. The separation into Halls, inevitable for a time, had, in Miss Clough's estimation and perhaps in reality, a very decided advantage. Students in one Hall naturally saw more of one another than of those in other Halls; Old Hall especially was somewhat cut off from the two others, so long as the public road ran between. And for games, clubs, and other social purposes, it was often a help to have a natural division into the three Halls. The larger societies—such as the Debating Society, the Musical Society, and some others, as well as the more regular of the Games Clubs—belonged to the College as a whole. The teaching arrangements were, of course, always made for the whole College and not separately for each Hall.

From about this time the social activities of the students, both those resident in College and those who had gone back to their own homes or taken up definite work, showed themselves in many ways. In 1880 an effort was made to keep up in those who had gone down the College spirit and College interests. The result was a society called the Newnham College Club, rather an unfortunate name, since it was not a club properly so-called, having no local habitation ; it sometimes became confounded with the Ladies' University Club, and students were debarred from entering by the fear of expense. The " Club " prepared students' minds for the official College Roll which superseded it in 1919. The founders and officers of the Club (among whom those especially active in its initiation and development were Miss Julia Sharpe, Miss Olive Macmillan (Mrs. MacLehose), Mrs. Corrie Grant (*née* Adams), deserve the gratitude of the College for having, by means of an annual *Newnham Letter*, with information as to College developments, births, marriages, deaths among old students, fresh appointments, etc., and by regular meetings in London, kept alive in a large and growing number of former students the memory of their Alma Mater and her interest in the doings of her children. In after times it was interesting to see how, when a member of the Club who had gone to live in Central Africa or New Zealand visited her old haunts, she was found to be far better informed as to the lines of recent progress than some who had never left England.

In another direction Newnham took the lead, this time on the direct initiation of Miss Clough, in the formation of a teachers' agency for qualified women who had taken a College course. The governesses' agencies of those days opened their doors to stronger and to feebler applicants. Heads of schools and families desiring well-educated teachers were constantly writing to Miss Clough, and it seemed time to start a registry on collegiate lines. She communicated the project to a few former students engaged or interested in education, and they at once formed a committee, invited the co-operation of Girton, the Oxford Colleges, and the graduated women of London University, and started what became the Association of University Women Teachers. From ten or a dozen members it has increased to over 2800. The idea of this Society, as compared with the ordinary registry, was that the Secretary, a University woman and in close touch with Universities, should keep herself personally informed as to the credentials and careers of applicants ; that she should make sure of the eligibility of the posts offered ; and that she should be able to offer advice to young teachers as to applying for posts and making changes when, but not before, it seemed expedient ; and that the expenses should, as far as possible, be defrayed from the ordinary subscriptions of members. Further, and this was a point of much importance, it was intended that the Association should watch over the interests of women teachers, and should interest itself in educational questions generally. The secretaryship has been held by various University women—for many years by Miss Alice Gruner, whose experience and untiring devotion to the work made her a most valuable adviser both to those who offered and those who were seeking educational posts. It is now filled by Mrs. Brough (*née* Lloyd), and has offices at 108 Victoria Street, Westminster.

Miss Clough never lost her interest in school teaching and teachers, of any and all types. At one time she arranged for parties of Newnham students to visit some of the elementary schools in Cambridge and give amateur lessons—chiefly that they might know what the inside of an elementary schoolroom was like—partly because, as she entirely believed, education and mutual acquaintance are the great factors for breaking down class distinctions. Meantime, a body of energetic Newnham students (led by Miss E. P. Hughes, Miss A. M. Adams and others) were eager to help in the education of working men. For many years a school was kept up in St. Matthew's Schoolroom, Barnwell,

for men who were known not to go to church on
Sunday mornings, but who wished, during those
hours, to learn some of the elements which—in
those days—many adults had never acquired.
Miss Clough was much interested in the scheme,
and once or twice came down to speak to the men,
though she was anxious that no student should, in
taking part in the work, give up time that she
required for Sunday rest. The school was for
some years vigorously carried on by the late Principal, Miss Stephen. While it lasted, it certainly
did good work on both sides. The classes were
conversational, and many students learned at least
something of working men's life and ambitions.
It died down partly owing to the irregularity necessitated by the alternation of terms and vacations,
partly to the activities of a new clergyman, who
was not without hope of inducing men to go to
church on Sunday mornings.

The interest which Miss Clough always felt, and
which she imparted to a good many students, in
elementary teachers and their work was shown in
certain experiments, novel as they seemed then,
though precursive of greater things. She was
anxious that those teachers who had a hard and
often a dull life, and whom she knew to be often
most conscientious and zealous in their profession,
should see something of a different life, and especially of University life, and in particular that they

should enjoy some rambles among the old Colleges of Cambridge, and hear lectures from Cambridge teachers. The Summer Meeting of the Extension Scheme was not as yet, unless one counts it as beginning in these Newnham gatherings. Certainly it originated in the circle of educational pioneers to which Miss Clough belonged, and some of the earliest " Extension Students " were successors to those who had come up under the early scheme. In the summer of 1885 two men and two women from the northern counties (the women being both elementary teachers) received bursaries from the Lectures Association in the north that they might come for three or four weeks' study in Cambridge. The women were accommodated in Newnham, and though their teaching had been otherwise provided for, Miss Clough commended them to the care of some of the younger lecturers, who did the chaperoning required in those more exacting days, and gave what social and friendly help was required. In 1887 Miss Clough undertook a similar experiment on her own account. A party of about fourteen women teachers in elementary schools were accommodated for three weeks in the Red Houses which formed the interim abode of students while Clough Hall was in process of building and were not required during the Long Vacation. In 1889 and 1891 the experiment was repeated, the teachers being received into the Old Hall. Certain of the younger

lecturers gave them lectures in History and Literature, and in some of the subjects (Latin, Logic,
etc.) with which they were struggling for their
examinations, while the Natural Science lecturers
took several of them into the laboratories and for
botanical excursions. The lecturers and students
of Newnham acted up to the College reputation for
hospitality, and Miss Clough herself visited them
and invited them to see her in her private room.
The grievances of teaching in the days of half-time
pupils and dearth of money and books for teachers
were poured into sympathetic ears. After the
Annual Summer Meeting of University Extension
Students had been fairly set on foot these sectional
meetings became merged in the general one, and
there was no need for such special gatherings at
Newnham, but the College, when the Meeting was
in Cambridge, has always received a number of
Extension Students as paying guests, and lecturers
and other Newnham officials have taken pains to
make the visit profitable, so that many came year
after year and always cherished an affection for
Newnham above and beyond that which they felt
for Cambridge.

This movement was one from above—originated
by the Principal and worked mainly by the Staff.
But the one which brought Newnham generally most
closely into contact with what one may call socio-
educational work was the Women's University

MRS. HENRY SIDGWICK.

From the portrait by J. J. Shannon, R.A.

Settlement in Southwark. The idea of "settlements" is familiar nowadays, and the original character and object of such institutions has much changed and developed since the first experiment was begun by the inspiration and intense activity of Arnold Toynbee. The primary notion of a *settlement* was of an abode in the poorer districts of a town where men of culture, engaged in various occupations, might make their home, devoting their leisure to the society and to the amusement or assistance of poorer neighbours. While this ideal is more or less preserved in the numerous settlements—some connected with particular churches or colleges, others quite independent—to be found in London and in others of our big towns, perhaps the possibility of uniting outside professional duties in the daytime with attention to social evils and their remedies in the evenings has not been permanently realized in any. Certainly in Settlements of women, the self-regarding part of the work has become chiefly educational : the training of the worker by instruction in the principles of economics and the history of social legislation. The Settlement in Southwark was throughout of this description. Though it has been carried on by women from other Universities as well as Cambridge women, the first thought of such an enterprise arose in Cambridge after an interesting meeting of the Society for Discussing Social Questions. This society of

Cambridge ladies, including Girton and Newnham students (founded chiefly by the efforts of Mrs. Marshall), held, Feb. 4th, 1887, an interesting meeting at which Mrs. Samuel Barnett, wife of the Warden of Toynbee Hall, and Miss Alice Gruner—lately a historical student of Newnham College—read interesting papers on *Settlements*. Miss Gruner had already begun work of the kind in London and was anxious to find helpers. Several students were inspired to initiate a Settlement; Miss Gruner consented to allow her undertaking to be taken over as the nucleus and became the first Warden. Girton was appealed to and also the Oxford Halls. The result was the formation of a Committee and the acquiring of a house in Nelson Square, London, S.E., Miss Gruner having laid her finger on the very spot afterwards marked most darkly in Sir C. Booth's *Life and Labour of the People*. The history of the Settlement, the development of its various activities, the links which it formed with other agencies, religious and secular, in combining for the betterment of conditions among the London poor, the schemes adopted by its residents and afterwards taken up by public authorities, do not belong, except indirectly, to the history of Newnham College, yet the Settlement has certainly been a factor in the life of many students, and it is not too much to say that what was first discussed within the walls of Newnham has been successfully worked out in many parts of England and, indeed, in some distant lands. Many University women besides Newnham students have worked there, and one may suppose that in a sense the movement was " in the air " and would in any case have come into active existence. Yet Newnham may enjoy some of the credit of the work done in Southwark and of the excellent Wardens provided in the persons of Miss Gruner, Miss Sewell, Miss Gladstone, and the present head, Miss M. M. Sharpley. Workers and officers of much devotion and ability have been supplied by Oxford and the London University and Settlements of a somewhat similar kind form adjuncts to other Universities, such as Bristol, Leeds and Birmingham.

If Newnham was making its way, as learner, as teacher, and as worker, in the field of social enterprise, the same is even more true in that of education. A large proportion of the students during the time now under consideration adopted the teaching profession. Technical training was not insisted on by head mistresses, nor by the Government, and most young women plunged into educational life to sink or swim—some of those who might have sunk emerging after a term or two to take a course of training. The head for many years of the Maria Grey Training College was a University woman (Miss Alice Woods of Girton) and the first head of

the Cambridge Training College was from Newnham—Miss E. P. Hughes. Meantime, the standard
of attainment in girls' schools was rapidly rising,
as women who had received a University education
took up posts in them and imbued their pupils with
a desire to come up some day to Cambridge. At
first, former students had often to work as assistants
under Heads of a different and older type, but this
was not always a disadvantage, as the older, partly
self-taught, mistresses, both of public and private
schools, sometimes showed an admirable power
of blending the new life which young University teachers brought into the schools with
the good traditions of the last generation. In
course of time head mistresses were generally
appointed from assistants who had a good " degree
or its equivalent," and the bonds between schools
and the University thus became stronger.

In 1890 the College had again a festive occasion—
on the attainment by Miss Philippa Fawcett of a
place in the Mathematical Tripos above the Senior
Wrangler. The scene in the Senate-house is one
that will live in the memory of all who were present.
It is pleasant to be able to say that no discord-
ant note was struck. As Miss Fawcett passed out,
with Miss Clough leaning on her arm, the undergraduates formed a line on either side and gave a
hearty cheer. The event was celebrated at Newnham
by a dinner in Hall, at which Mrs. Fawcett was

present, and also Dr. Hobson, Miss Fawcett's tutor in mathematics. In the evening her student friends decorated the doorway with lamps, and as there was just then a piece of waste ground at the west-end of the College grounds, it was possible to make a bonfire, and to carry the Senior Wrangler round it, and in the light of the fire to call on Dr. Hobson for a speech. Miss Clough was quietly happy, and all present felt that there was something of poetical justice in the occurrence. Professor and Mrs. Fawcett had been, as we have seen, pioneers in the movement for women's education; they had also been warmly attached to Miss Clough, as, in a more filial way, their daughter had been for many years. Miss Fawcett herself, besides being one to whose brilliant mathematical powers the highest academic honours were due, was a singularly suitable person for this high distinction, in that she exemplified so many of the qualities popularly supposed to be absent from the character of a University woman. She was modest and retiring, almost to a fault—trying though not always successfully, to counteract the impression made by her personality, so as to appear like a very ordinary person—not known to many, but loved as well as admired by her intimate friends. As the subsequent career of Miss Fawcett is not well known, it may be stated here that after the second and more advanced part of the Mathematical Tripos (in which she obtained the highest honours) she held for a year the Marion Kennedy Studentship already referred to, and wrote on a problem involving advanced mathematical research. She subsequently acted as Mathematical Lecturer at Newnham, but feeling, as her father had felt before her, the call of national service above all inducement to academic pursuits, she accepted a Government appointment and went out to help organize education in the Transvaal. After a period of assiduous work in Johannesburg, she returned to England and was appointed a Principal Assistant in the Education Department of the London County Council, a post of much importance and responsibility. Miss Fawcett served for some years on the Council of Newnham College, and has maintained a constant interest in its welfare.

To return to the history of the College : in February 1892 it had to sustain a loss which was hardly less a blow from having come in the ordinary course of nature. Miss Clough was 72 years old in the January of that year. She had to most people looked about the same age for many years, as her hair had whitened early, and the vivid look in her eyes never suggested old age. The portrait of her by Shannon, painted in 1890, gives a better impression of her than Richmond's portrait of 1882.[1]

---

[1] Now hanging in the Old Hall Library. The expression is stern, and it was caricatured in *Punch* as " The very ready letter-writer ; won't I give it him ? " She remarked to a former

The latter shows, perhaps, more strength, the former more sweetness. But neither can possibly give an adequate interpretation to a face so speaking and changeful. Shannon's is a sympathetic study of calm, benevolent, but alert old age, suggestive of ripe experience and of a patient outlook on life. It hangs in the College Hall with the portraits of Prof. and Mrs. Sidgwick and Miss Kennedy, all of them pleasing and profitable reminders to the students, at their meals, debates, and dancing, of the character as well as the appearance of those to whom they owe their present happy opportunities.

During the later part of her life Miss Clough had been obliged to let some of her work be lightened, and to give the management of Clough Hall to Miss Katharine Stephen, who had formerly been Miss Gladstone's secretary ; but she still kept an eye on everything that happened in the College, and many things far beyond. Miss Clough had always felt a deep interest in the colonies, and she kept up a correspondence with past students who had made educational ventures in many distant parts. As one of them said, " her interest in us seemed to vary directly as the squares of the

student that she wished she could have had some young friends to talk to whilst it was being painted. " But didn't the artist talk to you, Miss Clough ? " " Yes, on subjects as to which we did not agree."

distances," though certainly those nearer to Cambridge would not have accepted such a formula. Such schemes as the mixed education for blacks and whites in Jamaica, the starting of a loan library in tropical Australia, the opening of a boarding-school for aristocratic girls in Siam, aroused her warm interest and often called forth wholesome advice as well as sympathy. She was always able to enjoy a quiet country holiday in vacation time. The pleasures of friendship brought her comfort and enjoyment all her life, during the latter part of which she had the companionship of her niece—daughter of the brother to whom she had owed so much in her early intellectual development—and much care and solicitude from some of the lecturers and of the elder students. She may be said to have died in harness. The last time that she appeared at a meeting for students was to interest them in Mr. Morant's educational efforts in Siam. One of the last visitors from abroad whom she received, lying on a sitting-room couch, was a lady from Australia who could bring tidings of a University hostel managed by a former student. Miss Clough was not sure that this student was working on the best lines, and was anxious to hear about her and to send her a message of kindly warning.

The end came quietly on February 27th, 1892. To very many it seemed as if the world could never be quite the same without her. Certainly the

College, however wisely and generously conducted, was bound to follow new courses. Yet in a sense Miss Clough was *felix opportunitate mortis*. She had lived to see her work set on a stable footing ; she might safely leave it in the hands of those like-minded with herself ; and she was spared the pain of friction and later of bitter opposition which the College and its promoters had to suffer in seeking a permanent place within University borders.

Miss Clough's kinsfolk showed great breadth of mind, generosity, and appreciation of her own desires and feelings, in arranging that the funeral should be rather of a collegiate than of a family character. She had expressed a wish that her remains should rest in a churchyard rather than a cemetery, and as she possessed a little property in the parish of Grantchester, the burial was in the pleasant ground attached to the church there. A simple slab was afterwards erected with name, date, and the words : " After she had served her generation by the will of God, she fell on sleep." The first part of the service was, by the kind offer of the Provost and Fellows of King's College, read in the beautiful chapel of that College, the services of which had been to her, for many years, a perpetual solace and aid. The Staff of Newnham walked behind the coffin. The Chapel was crowded with members of the University and a great number of former students from all parts of England. The following Sunday (the First in Lent) it fell to Dr. Ryle (now Dean of Westminster) to preach a sermon, and the subject suited to the season and also to Miss Clough's character and work suggested his text : " Endure hardness, as a good soldier of Jesus Christ." His reference was very appreciative and delicate. Perhaps it might have struck some hearers that though Miss Clough would have thoroughly appreciated the idea of service in the Christian army, she might not have considered that she had " endured hardness " as much as many others. Her strenuous efforts and personal restrictions were so entirely dictated by the needs of her cause and of the individuals in her charge, that there was no place for asceticism in her life, though much for plain living and high thinking.

The figure of Miss Clough must necessarily look large in the history of Newnham College, since she was both its principal founder and its first head. But it would be useless labour to compare her with other founders and heads. Her objects and her way of obtaining them were peculiar to herself in her particular *milieu*. When she was removed, others who had supported her were ready to follow up her work, perhaps on more consistently stated principles, with somewhat more of theory in the background. But there were some ideas at the basis of the College recognised only by those who had caught her spirit, either by working under her in life or by imbibing the moral and intellectual atmosphere which for a long time has kept the College sound and wholesome. The mental and moral debt of the present College to her, and to those one may call her disciples, has been more or less manifest already, and will appear more evident in the sequel.

CHAPTER IV

NEWNHAM COLLEGE IN PROGRESS, 1892-1911— PRINCIPALSHIP OF MRS. SIDGWICK.

THE loss of Miss Clough seemed to remove the College from its early—one might say heroic— period to the regions of ordinary history. Yet there was something uncommon in the circumstances under which her successor was appointed. At the Council Meeting after Miss Clough's death, a strong wish was expressed that Mrs. Sidgwick, who had already once given up, with her husband, the privacy of home life, might be induced to become the second Principal. Newnham wanted them, and they came ; making, as one would expect, the very least of any personal inconvenience involved in once more giving up their house. As Sidgwick said to a friend,[1] " What we feel most strongly is that after Miss Clough's death it is the duty of all who have given their minds to Newnham to ' close ranks,' and take the place that others assign to one. We hope it will be for the good of the College."

[1] *Life*, p. 515.

For a short time Mrs. Sidgwick was obliged to live a divided life, part at Hillside, part at Newnham. But in December 1893 the Principal's new quarters were ready, and she and her husband moved into them.

These new quarters had been partly provided by a very timely bequest. A short time before, Mrs. Emily Pfeiffer, the poetess, and her husband, visited Cambridge, and were much pleased with what they saw of Newnham and with the hospitality of Miss Clough. Mrs. Pfeiffer died soon after, and her husband did not long survive her. Their money was left in great part to societies and buildings for the benefit of women, and of this the sum of £5000 was adjudged to Newnham College. There were some legal difficulties, soon overcome, but a hindrance remained in the fact already mentioned, that a public pathway divided Sidgwick Hall with Clough Hall from the Old Hall.

What was desired was to connect the two parts of the College by a block of buildings containing students' rooms, and, as finally arranged, a suite of rooms for the Principal, a set of small lecture or " coaching " rooms, a large room for the Staff, to serve as a kind of Combination Room, and a Porter's Lodge. This could not be done without closing the public foot-path. Fortunately, a new carriage road parallel to the former foot-path was greatly needed for communication between the town and the country beyond the College.   Such a road, if made, would compensate the public for the loss of the foot-path.   Newnham College was naturally willing enough to give up a strip along the north side of its grounds as a contribution to the road.   But others were less willing to give up portions of their ground, without which the scheme could not have been carried through.   After much discussion, a very satisfactory solution was reached.   A broad road, now called *Sidgwick Avenue,* was made, largely at the expense of Professor and Mrs. Sidgwick, with some help from other friends, and the path was closed.   There was a curious interregnum, after the dividing fences of the Hall gardens had been removed and before the path had become private, during which tradesmen's boys used to loiter, basket on head, as they passed through to the Grange Road, and watch the students' games at hockey or tennis.   When Sidgwick Avenue was complete and the path closed, this anomaly naturally ceased.

In the archway under Pfeiffer Building, forming the main entrance to the College, were placed a pair of beautiful bronze gates.   These were presented by past and present students, in memory of Miss Clough.   They bear the Clough Arms, and the decoration is a combination of floral and foliate. The designer was the architect of all the College buildings, Mr. Basil Champneys.   It was said at

NEWNHAM COLLEGE—THE ENTRANCE GATES.

the preliminary meeting that in future every student would have Miss Clough brought to her mind on her first entry into the College and her departure from it. Unfortunately this cannot be carried out in practice, for though the Gates are the only means of ingress or egress after dark and form the principal entrance to the College as a whole, there are other entrances to three of the Halls which are used by day.

Thus the suite of rooms above the Memorial Gates formed the dwelling-house of Professor and Mrs. Sidgwick, a somewhat inadequate " Master's Lodge " for a large and rising College, but pleasant in outlook and sufficient in size for all immediate requirements. Needless to say, the hospitable traditions of Hillside were maintained at Newnham, and members of the Staff had opportunities of occasionally meeting very interesting guests who came from far and near.

The Principal's life was a full one. Besides being Principal of the College she was its Bursar—an office which she only resigned at the end of 1919, to the regret of those who realized how much the financial success of the College has owed to her care and thought. Careful and even abstemious in all personal expenditure, she was always ready to entertain suggestions of new ventures. But besides this, she kept an eye on everything that happened in the College. She took all opportunities of coming to know the students personally, by frequently dining in hall, inviting students to her drawing-room and to breakfast, attending debates and little entertainments, and by making the College, both during her husband's lifetime and afterwards, an evidently large factor in her life. His presence, while he lived in the background, was always a help and a stimulus. If he made sacrifices in giving up his private house, he made many more in the time he devoted to the College at large and to students in particular. But with him and his wife, as with the first Principal, such sacrifices were so much the order of the day as hardly to be recognized as such, and were only fully appreciated in later years.

One sacrifice made by Mrs. Sidgwick for the good of the College was the restriction of the time she could now give to the work of the Society for Psychical Research. She maintained the interest she and her husband had long felt in the Society, and took part in its meetings and various proceedings. But she never encouraged such interest among the students, since she knew how many unsteady heads have been turned by a superstitious dabbling in the occult. It would be difficult to over-estimate the advantage to the Society of having persons of such complete sanity and scrupulous balance of mind as the Sidgwicks among the investigators.

We have noticed as one of the additions to the College in connection with the Pfeiffer Building a Combination Room for the Staff, including all women Lecturers and resident Fellows. Later on its functions were transferred to its present quarters, the room next the College Dining Hall—a pleasant room with two fireplaces and a door opening on the garden—the original Combination Room being made use of partly as a committee room, partly as a reading and coaching room for students.

Work among both students and past students had meantime been facilitated by the gift in 1898 of a well-designed library building, for which the College has to thank the liberality of Mr. and Mrs. Yates Thompson. The Library is admirably adapted to its purpose, with section recesses divided off by bookcases and conveniently arranged tables, while beauty of proportion, the excellence of the woodwork, and the elaborate mouldings on the ceiling (of the principal Printers' Arms of the sixteenth century) give it an artistic as well as academic character. When (1907) nearly ten years after its opening, its space proved insufficient for the books belonging to the College, the same benefactors most generously doubled it in size, providing staircases and a fine east window.

The supply of library books grew and prospered at least in proportion to the general progress of the College. Many of the original promoters were literary men and book-lovers, and their gifts and bequests, besides the money annually spent out of the College income, made the necessary extension just noticed necessary, and tended to make the College a more desirable place for old students— especially such as were engaged in educational or literary work—in which to spend part of the summer vacation. Some friends were anxious that the Library should have interesting books of a non-special character. Mrs. Stephen Winkworth, already mentioned, whenever she had enjoyed some new work of biography or general literature, used to send a copy of it for the Newnham Library. Mr. Coutts Trotter, Miss Clough's kind adviser in the early days, bequeathed the bulk of his books to Newnham College. The same was done by Mary Bateson, of whom we shall have more to say presently. There never was a time when there was not an influx of books of various kinds. Provision was made for a steady supply by the assignment to the Library Committee every year of a sum proportional to the number of students. Most books, on conditions, might be taken out for parts of the vacations. The Library Committee consists of representatives on the Staff of all the principal subjects studied and other lecturers, whose duty it is to submit the names of books required by the students whom they direct. The Library has thus been kept up to date, and has also continually been enriched by special gifts. Thus a Dante Library was formed in memory of Miss Jane Lee, already mentioned ; a clock was given by a generation of students going down, the case being designed by one of them ; guests gave books on their departure. The catalogues were carefully kept, and if any slackness in returning books was observed, great vigilance was used to recall them. The care of the Library was for many years in the hands of Miss Katharine Stephen.

It had been the wish of early friends—especially of Miss Kennedy—to attach permanently to the College as many as possible of the past students. This had been done to a certain extent, as already shown, by the Newnham College Club. Another plan, still adhered to, is to invite all students who belonged to specified periods, to come up to Commemoration Dinner on or about February 24th— a practice more or less observed in the Colleges of the University. But in addition it was the aim of the founders to bring the old students into the Constitution, so that the responsibility for the College should eventually be to a greater extent in their hands. With this object in view, the Constitution was revised, and in 1893 a new body of members was created chosen from the old students and called Associates (not Associate Members, who were a separate class of members qualified by subscriptions). In this year all past students were

requested to send in the names of those twenty
among their College contemporaries or friends
whom they considered most fitted to aid the causes
of " Education, learning, and research." To the
first twenty who obtained the greatest number of
votes the Council added ten, and the number was
increased by annual election of three till it reached
48, after which time three were to resign every year
and three others to be chosen by co-optation. The
Associates were full members of the College, and
as such took part in the election of the Council,
and still, under the later Constitution, elect members
of the Governing Body. They meet in Cambridge
every year, and coming as they do from various
centres, contribute new ideas and points of view.
At first, as might naturally be expected, most of
the resident Staff were placed on the list. It
includes many women who have reached some degree
of eminence in their several lines of activity and
also usually some research fellows.

There was in these years a growing desire to
provide opportunities for what may be called post-
graduate work, though the term is not strictly
applicable. There had been, as we have seen,
students doing advanced work before the foundation of any research fellowships. The studentship
connected with the name of Miss Marion Kennedy
had given opportunity for a successful Tripos
student to look about her, try some manageable

piece of work, and either find some fresh line to follow up in the field of science or letters, or else enter the teaching profession with a wider view of her functions than could generally be found in one who had never advanced in her studies beyond the undergraduate stage. Studentships in the Natural Sciences were, from 1881, awarded from time to time to students of post-graduate status from the Bathurst Fund already mentioned. But something involving a longer period of independent study was clearly desirable. Critics of the women's education movement were wont to assert that women might do fairly well in Triposes and in educational work afterwards, but that they contributed nothing of any significance to the advancement of knowledge. This " hasty generalization " needed removing. It was, however, no mere spirit of feminine rivalry, but a generous impetus to labour in intellectual fields, to satisfy one's own thirst for truth, and to help in the building up of the sciences—whether natural or human—that inspired the promoters and labourers in this new field of College activity. The most eager and influential in this movement was a member of the College eminently marked by a keen delight in research for its own sake, and by a desire that Newnham should be able to hold its own in the highest kind of University work among all the Colleges of the world—Mary Bateson. Under her influence the

first research fellowship was given by Mrs. Herring-
ham, and was thrown open to public application in
1900. Friends of the College and the students
themselves were stirred up to raise funds for more
research fellowships. The number is now four, and
they are awarded by a special committee and tenable
for three years. The stipend was originally sufficient to pay the expenses of a woman resident in
the College, though a small amount of lecturing or
tuition was held to be compatible with the duties
of the fellow.[1] The first Newnham students to hold
a research fellowship were Miss J. E. Harrison and
Miss G. L. Elles (1900). The former had already
acquired celebrity by her archaeological works—
especially her *Myths and Monuments of Ancient
Athens*—and had been invited to occupy rooms in
Newnham, where she speedily created a keen
interest among students and many of the Staff,
first in classical archaeology and later in anthro-
pology. Miss Elles is well known as a geologist,
and had already been teaching at the Sedgwick
Museum under Professor Hughes.

With the research fellowships it has been possible to retain at Newnham advanced students
whose researches have made a solid contribution to
knowledge. Though it may seem invidious to

[1] But owing to the depreciation of money these stipends have
become inadequate, and unless the endowment can be increased
the number of research fellows will have to be diminished.

make a selection, mention may be made of the researches of Miss E. R. Saunders (partly in co-operation with Mr. Bateson) into the laws of Variation ; the study of floral pigments by Miss Wheldale (Mrs. Onslow) ; that of animal psychology by Miss E. M. Smith (Mrs. Bartlett) ; and in widely different fields, Miss Maud Sellers' valuable work in rescuing and making public the records of the Merchant Adventurers of York ; that of Miss Paues, in unearthing a Middle-English Bible ; Mrs. Temperley's (*née* Bradford) studies in Tudor Proclamations and other legal antiquities ; and, not least, the wide range of Miss Mary Bateson's work in Mediaeval History, chiefly monastic and municipal.

Mary Bateson was so much the prime mover in the development of Newnham work for the advancement of learning, and some of the teachers who stimulated and directed her efforts were so evidently epoch-making in the lives of Newnham students ; also her tragically sudden death in 1906 cut short such a remarkably promising career and evoked so much sympathy with Newnham throughout the University, that a few more words may be devoted to keeping her memory fresh. Her father (Master of St. John's College) and her mother—much distinguished in her zealous efforts for the betterment of women—were old friends of Miss Clough and the College ; her elder brother, Mr. William Bateson, is well known for his remarkable work on heredity. Mary Bateson began independent research in the Monastic Civilisation of the Fens, even before she took the Historical tripos, in which she naturally obtained a good first class. Her literary activity in the production of articles for learned periodicals, and later very substantial books, was immense. At the same time, her zeal in the cause of her own College never faltered. For many years she was ready to do what teaching was offered to her on her own lines, and she did it exceedingly well. But her great task in the College was to produce a noble discontent. She cared far less that the students should take good places in their examinations than that they should come to understand what sound learning really means, and should share her own delight in the search for undiscovered truth. Broad in her sympathies with all honest workers, genial in her manners, remarkably constant and helpful in her friendships, and withal scholarly to the backbone in her tastes and ambitions, she stands out as one of the leading figures of our College. Two main influences determined her course : first, that of Professor Creighton, afterwards Bishop of Peterborough and subsequently Bishop of London, who came to Cambridge in 1885, and began a new departure in History of the kind that appealed to Mary Bateson's mind and character. She became attached to his family, and he inspired her with the ambition which he felt for himself when he prescribed for his epitaph the words, "He tried to write true history." After Dr. Creighton's departure from Cambridge, the teacher from whom she derived most inspiration and with whom she sometimes collaborated was the distinguished writer, Professor F. W. Maitland—also a most effective teacher and helper of historical students at Newnham and in the University generally. Miss Bateson's researches into *Borough Customs*, as well as her previous volumes on the *Records of the History of Leicester*, earned her an honourable place among standard historians of mediaeval institutions, while her small book on *Mediaeval England*, and her admirable account of the " Colonization of Canada " in the seventh volume of the *Cambridge Modern History*, may always be recommended confidently to the general reader. Mary Bateson was deeply interested in politics and a strong advocate for women's suffrage, on behalf of which, in a deputation to the then Prime Minister (Sir H. Campbell-Bannerman), she made an exceedingly able and trenchant speech. But she cared far more that women should progress in knowledge and capacity than in political power. The great esteem in which she had been held was shown in the large attendance of University men and former students at the funeral service in St. John's Chapel, and in the readiness with which the proposal was received, at

G

a meeting in St. John's in the following May, of a
memorial to her in Cambridge, which took the
appropriate form of an additional Research Fellowship. This fellowship bears her name, and is
generally—*ceteris paribus*—given to a former student
engaged in some branch of historical research.

An earlier loss—happily not so permanent—
was sustained in 1896 when Miss Gladstone, owing
to the rapidly declining health of her father,
felt bound to resign her College post for family
duties. Miss Gladstone had not only, as already
shown, become a most valuable element in the life
of the College by her geniality and devotion to the
duties she had undertaken. She also, in the eyes
of the world, raised the reputation of the College,
since an institution must be of *some* significance if
the daughter of one of the most eminent men in
the country, having access to the most brilliant
and interesting society, thought it worth while to
give up—for most of the year—the delights of such
an attractive home for the service of a College for
women.[1] Miss Gladstone had of late been not only
Vice-Principal (Tutor) in Sidgwick Hall, but
Secretary to the Education Committee, a position
which brought her into constant communication

---

[1] Mr. Gladstone twice visited his daughter in Newnham
College : once while he was out of office but intensely popular—
on which occasion he was entertained at a genuine students'
tea-party ; the second time when she was Vice-Principal in
Sidgwick Hall.

with most of the resident lecturers. In a sense, the loss could not be entirely repaired, though Miss Stephen succeeded her as head of Sidgwick Hall. Miss Stephen had originally come to Newnham as Secretary to Miss Gladstone, and had become very popular with the students, especially in helping in their political debates. She had also, as we have already said, the charge of the Library, in which she seemed to know the exact place of every important book. As she was a daughter of Sir James Fitzjames Stephen, the distinguished judge, and a niece of Leslie Stephen (who was induced more than once to come and give a delightful lecture to the students), she helped to continue the traditions of public and intellectual eminence which the students have always found in the records of their benefactors. In memory of Miss Gladstone's vice-principalship, the students raised money to build an annexe to the dining hall of Sidgwick Hall which, since the opening of a new wing in 1884, had proved insufficient for peace and comfort. Another and important addition to the College was the block named after others of the founders, Kennedy Buildings. Now that there were resident fellows and several research students, it was desirable that in some part of the College buildings there should be suites of two rooms, allowing more accommodation for books and more opportunities for entertaining than could be easily had in any of the three

Halls.   In 1899, through the remarkable generosity of several friends, the freehold of the land on which the College stands was bought.

But meantime, during a period of prosperity, Newnham had to experience its first serious set-back, a set-back only paralleled in the week during which these lines are being written : the Senate of the University of Cambridge refused a petition to grant to Girton and Newnham students who had been successful in the triposes the title of degrees.

The movement had mainly arisen in 1897 to meet a difficulty springing from the inability of the world to understand that a certificate stating that a woman had attained the standard required for a degree in honours is really as good a guarantee of attainments as the letters B.A. to which every poll man is entitled. The handicapping was serious. At the same time, more definite status was earnestly desired. The first suggestion of a granting of degrees was at once dropped. Various compromises were made by friends and opponents : in those of the former there was the suggestion of a titular B.A. and a real M.A. for women—too moderate and well reasoned to find many supporters. Another—widely taken up, but naturally unacceptable to all who were intimately and sympathetically concerned with higher education for women—was of a degree-granting University for women only, called in advance " The Queen's

NEWNHAM COLLEGE, 1920—GENERAL VIEW.

University," and styled by Professor Maitland in a brilliant speech on the other side as "Bletchley Junction Academy." This would have been even less of a real University than the original non-teaching University of London, since that at least had programmes of study and fixed standards, whereas the new one was to accept the standards of existing Universities. It is not certain, however, whether this impracticable scheme ever came into anything like definite form.

The Grace finally proposed by the second Syndicate appointed for the purpose was as follows :

"The University shall have power to grant by Diploma, Titles of Degrees in Arts, Law, Science, Letters, and Music to women who, either before or after the confirmation of this Statute, have fulfilled the conditions which shall be required of them for this purpose by the Ordinances of the University, and also shall have power to grant by diploma the same titles *honoris causa* to women who have not fulfilled the ordinary conditions, but have been recommended for such Titles by the Council of the Senate : provided always that a title granted under this section shall not involve membership of the University."

It was seen by many opponents and by some supporters that this Grace, if passed, would not have been a final settlement. But it would have removed an undoubted grievance. And in course of time, when the world had become accustomed to women vigorously and successfully engaged in the administration of colonial and provincial universities, full membership might have come in later without much controversy. The most striking speeches on the women's side were made by the late master of Trinity (Dr. Butler), Professor Maitland, Mr. (afterwards Professor) Bateson, and Professor Sidgwick. The speeches on the other side generally insisted, without much relevance, on the limitations of the female mind and the female physique, the impossibility of women's desire for University life and learning existing apart from a wish to copy and rival the other sex, and the like.[1] What the mind of Newnham, at its best, thought on the matter is ably expressed in a flysheet written by our Secretary, Miss Marion Kennedy, on the eve of the voting. I quote the later portion : " One appeal I should like to make to those whom we still regard as our friends, though for the moment they are opposed to us. It is that they may not be led to think that a separate University for women can be the true solution of the difficulty.

" Can we imagine what the position of such an institution would really be ? If it were merely a body for conferring degrees without holding examinations, its degrees must be given alike on the

---

[1] For the recommendations of the Syndicate and the chief speeches see *Cambridge University Reporter* for March 1st, 1897, and for March 26th, 1897.

examinations of Cambridge, Oxford, and Durham ; all the other Universities having opened their degrees. For the two latter I cannot judge, but I venture to ask any Cambridge man if he would care to bear a title which was given indiscriminately on the examination of his own University and on those of Oxford and Durham.[1] . . . If, on the other' hand, a Women's University held its own examinations, its standard could not possibly command the same respect as those of the older universities, nor could it give the inspiration which comes only of ancient tradition. As the Master of Trinity so well put it in his speech in the Senate House, generation after generation must be trained before any such comparison could be possible, and I fear the time must be measured not only by generations but by centuries. I think there is no doubt that if an attempt was made to found a Women's University, disappointment would be in store for any who would expect it to lay down a separate course or courses of study adapted to the supposed requirements of women. It would on the contrary be driven to follow the lines of the old University course even more closely than women are now required to do, as the only chance of giving its degrees any practical value. This leads to

[1] Of course now that Oxford and Durham admit women to degrees this argument cannot be transferred to the present crisis. (Dec. 1920.)

another point on which I think that a few of our opponents have not treated us quite fairly. It has been said that women wish to take the Cambridge course merely because they aim at imitating men. Surely this assumption is hardly justified by the facts. May it not be believed that women honestly seek to share what long experience has decided to be the best training for the mind?

" It seems to me we are far more likely to allow fair play to whatever mental differences exist between men and women by giving them impartially the best training and affording them every opportunity to develop their separate powers afterwards, than if we falsify the result through a diversity of training which must tend to obscure natural differences by overlaying them with artificial ones. I am well aware, however, that when all is said, differences of opinion will remain, and I only wish to express, once more, a hope that difference of opinion need not become intolerance ; that however this question is settled, we shall all be true to the noble and hitherto unbroken traditions of Cambridge that by-gones are by-gones, and that the morrow of a conflict here always finds victors and vanquished ready to join hands without any lessening of mutual regard and respect. Nothing would grieve me more than to have had any share in so carrying on the discussion as to render this more difficult.   MARION GRACE KENNEDY."

But for the time the voice of " sweet reasonableness " was drowned in angry clamour. Some
opponents of the College used their influence with
the undergraduates, and especially the athletic
element. Ridiculous stories were set about that
the women intended to press on to admission into
the Colleges. Aged and often very worthy men
who had long been out of touch with the University
but retained the right to vote in its proceedings
flocked up to " save the University " from the
dreaded feminine invasion. Friends of Newnham
and Girton mustered likewise, but the result was
obvious from the beginning. The motion was
defeated by 1713 to 662.

The set-back was felt severely, not so much by
reason of the weight of the adverse vote, as because
of the hostility that had unexpectedly come to the
surface, and the unmannerly way in which, led by
undergraduates' love of a " rag," it was manifested.
Happily, the feelings described by Miss Kennedy
were still characteristic of Cambridge, except in its
worse moments. Next term, when the Newnham
authorities came to discuss the wisdom of asking
lecturers who had taken the opposite part to continue their permission to women pupils, it was
found that some at least would have been indignant
if not asked to do so.

One good result of the unfortunate conflict
was that it brought the two women's Colleges,

Newnham and Girton, nearer together. There was generosity in the yielding by Miss Davies, Dr. Cunningham, and other notable supporters of Girton, of points which their Colleges had generally held with some tenacity. Newnham and Girton worked hand-in-hand during the conflict and in the steps by which the mischief done was gradually repaired.

Happily, since the generations of undergraduates and women students are short-lived, the episode became to many as if it had never been. This, however, was impossible in the case of the members of the resident staffs. It made, or should have made, each of them " a sadder and a wiser man " in future dealings with the University.

Before long Newnham had to suffer a greater loss, by the death of its protagonist in this and many other conflicts, as well as its ever-generous benefactor and friend : Professor Henry Sidgwick. Something has already been said both as to what he did and what he resigned for the good of the College, and yet more might be dwelt on as to the importance to students and staff of having him amongst them. Even those who were unable to appreciate the character of his mind, felt that he possessed a distinction they had known, if at all, in very few others. To those who attended his lectures, read his books, or listened to his talk, he was felt to excel all others in absolute devotion to truth and duty, in breadth of view, in moral and intellectual patience and forbearance, while this lofty character was always consistent with a keen sense of humour, and a human interest in all his surroundings. He had led an active life, though always liable to be troubled with insomnia. In May 1900, his doctor discovered an internal complaint which required an early operation. The operation was supposed to be successful, and after a short time he was able to go for drives and to enjoy the society of friends. But he was never deceived as to the nearness of the end, which came when he was staying with his brother-in-law, Lord Rayleigh, on August 28th, 1900. As it was mid vacation there was no funeral service in Trinity or elsewhere in Cambridge, but one attended by the family and a few friends in the church at Terling, in which churchyard he was buried.

It is, as already said, possible for all students to realize at once the benefits which the College owes to Sidgwick, and the greatness of his mind and character, by reading the life written by his wife and his brother Arthur. Very soon after the funeral Mrs. Sidgwick returned to Newnham, and the members of the Staff still in residence realized that this terrible loss to her did not involve the loss of her to the College, but that she would be to it at least all that she had been before.

A meeting was held soon after to decide how Professor Sidgwick should be commemorated in Cambridge. A University lectureship was founded with the proceeds of a general appeal, and a contribution to this was made from a special fund contributed by former students of Newnham ; this fund also provided for an annual Sidgwick Memorial Lecture at the College. The lecturer has in each case been appointed by Mrs. Sidgwick, and has generally so far been some man personally known to Dr. Sidgwick or interested in some of his own lines of thought. The first lecture was given by Professor (now Lord) Bryce in November 1902. His subject was " Philosophic Life among the Ancients," and many hearers felt—as did the lecturer himself—that the kind of life he was portraying had in no person been better exemplified than in Sidgwick himself. A visitor to Newnham afterwards, standing in the middle of the garden, quoted as appropriate to him the epitaph of Wren in St. Paul's : *Si monumentum requiris, circumspice.* But even that monument would be insufficient for those who had known something of his mind and profited by his labours.

CHAPTER V

PROGRESS, 1900-1914

THE years which elapsed between the death of
Professor Sidgwick and the retirement of Mrs.
Sidgwick from the principalship at the end of 1910
were marked by progress on various lines. The
increase of demand for accommodation led to the
building of a new Hall, with connecting passages,
at right angles to Clough Hall and Kennedy Buildings, and facing the Grange Road. This is on
much the same plan as the other Halls, with some
very pleasant common rooms, and accommodation
for another Vice-Principal (Tutor) and two lecturers, besides about fifty-six students. The central
kitchen, which—as already stated—helped greatly
to simplify and otherwise improve the domestic
arrangements, dates from the same time. Peile
Hall was named after Dr. and Mrs. Peile, whose
portraits hang in the dining-hall. Dr. Peile
died on the very day on which the Hall was
opened. It would be difficult to exaggerate
the value of the service rendered to the College

by Dr. Peile from its first beginnings till the day of his death.   He was constant in attending the Council, and was President for many years. His wisdom in giving advice in difficulties was equalled by his courage in defending the College in aspersions and attacks.   He had been an intimate friend of Professor Sidgwick and an eager promoter of University reform.   Mrs. Peile was intensely interested in everything connected with the College till the loss of her eyesight and her enfeebled health withdrew her from her former activities.

Another external addition to the College is the sunk garden, with fountain, in the lawn immediately opposite the Memorial Gates.   It was paid for as part of the memorial above mentioned by subscriptions of students past and present, and the stone margin has for legend : " The daughters of this house to those that shall come after commend the filial remembrance of Henry Sidgwick."

No further steps towards a request for degrees was made for many years after the rebuff in 1897, but in the spring of 1904 a recognition of the status of Tripos students came from an unexpected quarter —the University of Dublin.   There had been a party favourable to women graduates in Dublin, and the Royal University of Ireland already granted degrees to those women who had passed its examinations, among whom were the students of Alexandra College, the head of which had herself

been a Newnham student. After the death of a
very highly respected but also very conservative
Provost the authorities of Trinity College admitted
women to their degrees, and at the same time
offered an *ad eundem* degree to all women who had
passed examinations qualifying for a degree at
Oxford or Cambridge. Trinity College already
granted the *ad eundem* degree to graduates of
Oxford and Cambridge, and this new step amounted
to the recognition of the Tripos certificate granted
to women at Cambridge as the equivalent of a
degree. The result was perhaps surprising to its
originators, but not to those who really understood
one of the reasons why women students at Oxford
and Cambridge had asked for degrees. Numbers of
young women trooped over as soon as possible after
the results of their tripos were known, to take
the B.A. degree. Many others who if degrees
at Cambridge had been open to them would
have been of M.A. standing took B.A. and M.A.
both at Dublin. A few, whose literary or scientific
work had made them worthy of a doctorate, were
admitted to the higher degree. The Dublin officials
were apparently somewhat surprised and puzzled.
They generously applied most of the money raised
by fees to the establishment of a Hall of residence
for women students in Dublin.

This privilege was open to Oxford and Cambridge
women for a few years only, since the object which

the authorities of Trinity College, Dublin, had in view was to provide for those women who had begun or completed their courses elsewhere and could therefore not make use of the opportunities which the College now offered to women. One great advantage, however, had been derived by the general cause from the temporary grant of Dublin : it had been made clear that the degree of a respected University was, for women, really worth having. Busy women of moderate means do not take long journeys and pay considerable fees (£10 for the B.A. and £20 for the M.A.) for a merely fanciful advantage. Nor would the City Companies, which had granted certain scholarships to Newnham students, have been willing to pay, as they did, the fees for their scholars' Dublin degrees unless they felt sure that these would be to such scholars' advantage. A good many head mistresses felt it an advantage to be able to wear gown and hood, especially when some of their assistants could already wear the academic dress of London or of a Scotch or Welsh University. London did not grant its degrees to Cambridge women without some further test, though it admitted those who had taken Triposes to send in theses for a research M.A. degree without the actual B.A. degree required in men students. The only women who might have taken the Dublin degree, and had not much reason or inclination to do so, were members

MISS KATHARINE STEPHEN.

of the Newnham Staff, whose position was well understood by those around them. If, however, they migrated during the time that the Dublin *ad eundem* was open to them, they sometimes found it desirable to take it.

Mrs. Sidgwick's principalship came to an end in December 1910. Though Staff and students very deeply deplored her withdrawal, it was felt that she was more than entitled to more leisure for scientific pursuits, family enjoyments, and greater liberty generally. She was not lost altogether to Newnham, since she retained for several years the post of Treasurer (afterwards called *Bursar*), and after Dr. Peile's death she consented to become President of the Newnham College Council. The principalship was offered to Miss Katharine Stephen, who accepted it and held it for nearly ten years. Mrs. Sidgwick moved into a house separated from Peile Hall by the Grange Road only, and thus was easily in touch with College affairs.

One more improvement—and a very important one—was made before Mrs. Sidgwick's retirement : the determination of a fixed age for retirement for the Staff and of a pension to follow. The salaries of all the lecturers were raised and standardized. In the early days the pay had been low, even according to the standard of that time, simply because Newnham had not the funds at its disposal that better endowed Colleges possessed.

Still, as we have seen, a great deal had been done
for the promotion of learning and research, and
some of the lecturers had from time to time benefited
by the endowments for this purpose. But by the
arrangements which came into force in 1910 the
whole status and earnings of the Staff were revised,
and a contributory pension scheme initiated, with
a liberal provision for making the advantages of
the scheme retrospective in the case of lecturers of
some years' standing.

Shortly after these reforms, others on a larger
scale were projected, and in a few years successfully
accomplished. It was considered by some past
students that the Constitution of the College,
though it had worked well, was more fitted for the
infancy of such an institution than for its adult
life. The subject was naturally one taken up and
discussed by the Associates at their annual meeting.
Some Associates who were connected with one or
other of the provincial Universities were anxious to
introduce changes which would more or less assimi-
late Newnham to such Universities. Others held
that whatever changes were made ought to be
rather on a College than a University plan, and
that the wisest course would be to make Newnham,
in general government and arrangements, sufficiently like the Cambridge Colleges for it to be
able, if ever the happy day arose of its full recognition by the University, to fall into line and take

its place with the other Colleges. The Associates chose a committee from among themselves to draft a scheme, and to them were joined representatives of the Council, including experienced members of the University, who gave invaluable help, and the results they came to were successful in meeting with · a unanimous acceptance. The models chosen were chiefly the smaller Colleges, but none were followed slavishly, and the scheme when it emerged was found acceptable to the whole body of Associates. The Council on this, as on similar occasions, was not above taking suggestions from the past students and working on the lines thrown out. The result was a petition for a Charter which, with the Statutes of the College, became operative in the year 1917.

The main object of the Charter was to constitute " one body politic and corporate by the name and style of ' the Principal and Fellows of Newnham College ' " with perpetual succession, a common seal, power to sue and be sued in court, to hold and dispose of property and the like. Its chief objects were defined as : " (b) to establish and maintain at or near Cambridge a house or residence or houses or residences in which female students may reside and study ; (c) to provide a liberal education for women by carrying on the work of the old Association with such modifications as may from time to time appear desirable either in its present situation or elsewhere in the town of Cambridge or County of Cambridge ; (f) to do all such other things as are incidental or conducive to advancing education and learning among women in Cambridge and elsewhere."

One point with regard to the new Charter and Statutes requires notice, viz. the use of the name Fellow as applied to a member of " the one body politic and corporate." Hitherto the title of Fellow had been attached to the endowment for research for which funds had been collected as already mentioned. The word Fellow in the Cambridge Colleges had always connoted membership of a corporate body, but as Fellows of Colleges were in general chosen for academic eminence or promise the name was associated with the expectation of services in the advancement of learning and research. This association with the title had influenced the first champions of research for women, and in addition they desired that these endowments should be used by women of high standing and proved capacity in the sphere of learning to whom the status of Fellow rather than that of Research Student was due.

But when under the new Charter the constitution of Newnham was to some extent assimilated to those of the older Colleges, it seemed desirable that members of the new Governing Body should have the name which in Cambridge is associated with these functions. Therefore the name Fellow was given to members of the Governing Body, and that of Research Fellow to those who hold one of the special endowments for research. By the provisions of the Charter some of the Research Fellows must always be members of the Governing Body and therefore also Fellows.

To return to the government of the College as revised and established by the Charter :

The ultimate authority in the affairs of the College is the Governing Body. This comprises all full members of the Staff, a fixed number of Research Fellows chosen by the Governing Body ; representatives of the Associates,[1] and certain " Founders and Benefactors " living at the date of the Charter. The Council is a smaller body, and comprises besides the Principal, the Vice-Principal, the Bursar, and one of the Tutors, three members of the Senate of the University, elected by the Governing Body, seven additional members of the Governing Body, and three Founders and Benefactors alive in 1917.

Several points in the Charter will attract the attention of any student of former times who may be reading this history. The changes in nomenclature are, at first sight, puzzling. The use of the term *Fellow* has, as the most important, already been dwelt upon : that of *Tutor* as supplanting

[1] See p. 91.

Vice-Principal has also been noticed. There is now but *one* Vice-Principal, the numerous and important duties associated with the former vice-principalship being discharged by the Tutors superintending each Hall respectively. The Vice-Principal has now the functions properly assigned to the title, since she is bound to take the place of the Principal on necessary occasions, and especially to be in residence in the College when the Principal is absent (except in vacations). The term *Bursar* replaces that of *Treasurer*.

There is something of the nature of representative government in the election of Associate members on the Governing Body. The general body of past students has recognition in that the Statutes provide for the maintenance of a Newnham College Roll. The compiling and keeping up of this Roll has involved considerable labour on the part of the first registrar chosen to that office, Miss Edith Sharpley. It has, as already said, succeeded to the " Newnham College Club," but has recognised status. It now numbers a large proportion of former students, and the College may confidently look to them to further its interests and usefulness in all parts of the world.

Like the other Colleges, Newnham now has a Visitor, and the first Visitors have been two successive Chancellors of the University of Cambridge, Lord Rayleigh and the Rt. Hon. A. J. Balfour, respectively brother-in-law and brother of Mrs. Sidgwick.

Another feature in the new Constitution that will strike past students is the smaller proportion than formerly of members of the University compared to the Newnham College officials. It must not, however, be for a moment supposed that the College is not and will not continue to be in many ways dependent on the changes and general progress of the University. It will still be practically unable to take any important steps without the advice of some members of the University who are friendly to the College and its Staff. There will always be members of the Senate on the Council of Newnham College, and for some years, it is hoped, on the Governing Body. But beyond actual membership in any body concerned in the government of the College, Newnham must always hope to retain and even to increase the number of Cambridge dons and teachers interested both in its students, who may be their pupils, and in its lecturers, whom they regard as colleagues. In considerations of this kind, law can only create and maintain possible relations. The actual relations will, we trust, become modified as time goes on, and this, even in spite of temporary drawbacks, in the direction of closer co-operation and mutual respect between the men's and the women's Colleges in work and in other helpful intercourse.

From some provisions in the Charter, and from the general progress which has been traced, it must appear that the body of residents of graduate standing in Newnham, including administrative officials, lecturers, and Research Students· and Fellows, had for years been growing in importance and developing a corporate life. Junior to the Staff and Research Fellows, but of post-graduate standing, are those who hold the two or three research studentships which have been mentioned, and of late years others who have completed the degree courses have been enabled to stay on in Cambridge and carry on work in the laboratories by grants from the Medical Research Council and the Industrial Research Board. Of late, too, students with degrees from overseas and from other British Universities have come to Cambridge in increasing numbers to work for the recently established Research Certificates of the University. These students, with their wider interests and experience doing specialized advanced work in various subjects literary and scientific, some of them resident in the College, others living outside but connected with it, add a valuable element and form a link between the generations.

Old students are encouraged to come up to read in the Long Vacation, and thus keep up their old friendships and renew their old interests. Sometimes, it is true, Newnham is almost too full, with visitors from outside, to afford the peaceful time for uninterrupted and independent work characteristic of the " Longs " of former days. Yet the visits of distant friends is often stimulating as well as pleasant. Almost every other year, since the University Extension Summer Meetings began—we may almost say at Newnham's initiative [1]—some of the students have been accommodated in Newnham. This is true, too, of the Vacation Terms for Biblical Study ; since those were inaugurated by Mrs. Sidgwick's niece, Miss Margaret Benson, and intended chiefly as a help to school teachers, the promoters naturally looked to Newnham for hospitality, and many old students attend the courses. Learned societies of mathematicians, historians and others have often come to England from all over the world, and Newnham has been glad to entertain both learned ladies and the wives of learned men staying in the Colleges. Another kind of gathering may be mentioned, as somewhat original in idea and very useful in practice. Several of the students of Natural Science who, after taking their Tripos, had gone to teach in schools, complained of the scarcity and inferiority of the apparatus at their disposal. The lecturer in Chemical Science, Miss Ida Freund, arranged that a company of them should come to Cambridge for a part of the Long Vacation to learn how to

[1] See p. 71.

construct the simpler kind of instruments for themselves. The result was very satisfactory, and the teachers learned not only how to make the best of the conditions under which they might have to teach, but also how to keep abreast of the progress of the Natural Sciences and of the methods of teaching them. It seemed natural that on Miss Freund's lamented death in 1914 the Memorial to her should take the form of a brief course of lectures by an experienced teacher on the teaching of Physics. The summer meetings, at which these lectures were delivered, helped to keep teachers from falling behind in the general progress of knowledge and also to guide them in the practical work of education.

One very large part of the story of Newnham has been as yet little or incidentally treated in this history ; the development of student life and interests. At the beginning that was practically the whole life of the community : there were no dons, and the Principal (without losing separate and family interests) merged her life in that of the young people who were under her care. Things were bound to develop in both expected and unexpected ways. As more and more students came to College, variety increased, and at the same time College was likely to become more like a continuation of school. It would perhaps be impossible to trace quite accurately any particular tone or char-

acter or even standard of ability rising and falling
in the annals of the Newnham students. At first,
as already suggested, there was sure to be something of originality and enterprise. Girls were
never sent to College as a matter of course,
and in many cases they had had hard work in
persuading their parents to let them come even
for a slight taste of College life. Certainly some
came for a short spell and remained for many years,
though the fact of coming up without any definite
intentions often worked havoc with chances of
academic success. There were generally cultivated
adult women grappling with subjects which they
ought to have mastered in childhood ; and also
very young students striving after knowledge of a
kind beyond their present reach. Possibly these
aberrations made student life more interesting.
But they could not fail to be diminished—though
not even now eliminated—with the growth of a
more uniform standard in the curriculum of girls'
schools.

The oldest student society was the Debating
Society. It is said to have had its first meetings
under the medlar tree in Merton Hall garden. Its
rules were reduced to writing in the late seventies,
though subjected later to much revision. Its
history—like all histories—would, if written, show
great fluctuations in energy, popularity, and
capacity. In the early days there was quite enough

earnestness and desire to convince the world—the Newnham world that is—of the truth or falsity of certain propositions, political, moral or social. I believe that the good rule against reading speeches was generally adhered to, but it was sometimes avoided by the speech having been learned by heart, and having thereby lost spontaneity without acquiring the possible merits of a careful essay. The early generations of students were very kind and tolerant to wearisome speakers, though the time rule was strictly adhered to. The fatal fault of most debating societies—the desire to be humorous rather than convincing—threatened at times to destroy both qualities. But from time to time, capable speakers who really had something to say arose to retrieve the character of the Society. In 1884 it suffered somewhat by the creation of another society, which became almost co-extensive with the College, for discussing political questions. The original Debating Society did not preclude itself from politics, but it naturally left them to the other society, and was apt to descend to what was somewhat trivial or else took refuge in the paradoxical. Its temporary declines, however, were, as just said, generally followed by reinvigoration. Meantime the Political Debating Society, which met weekly (for the space of one hour only), kept up a very lively interest in public affairs, and also gave more practice in ready impromptu speaking than was possible in the general College debates. It adopted all the forms of an imitation House of Commons, with Speaker, Government, Opposition, and the like. Some older critics were only in part sympathetic, considering that the association of public interests with party disputes was detrimental to the formation of unprejudiced opinions. On the whole, however, the great advantage was secured of keeping a large number of students *au fait* with the chief political questions of the day. Additional instructiveness and liveliness were imparted by the fact that students whose fathers or friends were in Parliament occasionally " coached them up " in arguments and prognostications. The society became slack after many years, owing, I think, to the excessive burden thrown on a few students who were responsible for preparing the weekly business, and was reorganized with the forms of an ordinary debating society. It was suspended during the War, but revived—as society, not as amateur parliament—after the Armistice. It has since resumed the parliamentary form.

Besides the debating societies, each subject or group of subjects has for many years had its meetings for reading and discussing papers on Classical, Scientific, Historical, and many other subjects. Not infrequently some distinguished man or woman from outside has been invited to deliver a lecture.

The Choral Society began in the earlier days of Newnham, and long enjoyed the devoted and very able direction of Dr. Mann, Organist of King's College, and gave very successful concerts. The display of musical talent in the College is anything but uniform. One year we had a good orchestra of stringed instruments, and the same may occur again from time to time. Meanwhile, a musical society, started in a much humbler way by an industrious student who was desirous of "keeping up her practice" and inducing fellow students to do the same and be ready to play some piece to one another on Saturdays, has developed into a considerable College club called after its foundress, The Raleigh Musical Society. A good many students, too, have been members of the Cambridge University Musical Society.

Astronomical interests have been cultivated in non-mathematical students since the valuable gift of a telescope and small observatory by Mrs. Boreham (daughter-in-law of the astronomer) in 1891. It was at first placed on a mound to the south of Clough Hall, but when the view from it was obstructed by the building of Peile Hall it was removed to an open space at the far end of the College grounds. It was placed under the curatorship of a mathematical scholar who had not only been a high wrangler, but had had the advantage of having been brought up in an astronomical atmosphere, Miss E. A. Stoney. Students with no knowledge of astronomy were invited on certain evenings to see Saturn's rings and Jupiter's moons. Their interest was attracted even to things of the heavens which are visible to the naked eye. There was an enthusiasm for " learning the constellations," instruction being given by the expert to the ignorant. One night, when one of the mathematical lecturers informed the students that the phenomenon was about to take place described as " the Moon swallowing Jupiter," a large number of students assembled on the lawn to watch the event. Happily it occurred about 9 p.m. on a clear night. The act of swallowing was greeted by a cheer—though whether the object cheered was Jupiter, the Moon, or the lecturer who had given warning was not very clear. This little event is mentioned as one of the many cases in which the common life of students engaged in heterogeneous subjects has advantages of an educational as well as of a social kind.

We have already mentioned the lectures on Literature which were at one time given by first-rate men of letters to students of all faculties four or five times a year. Attendance at them was never compulsory, but the interest of the subject and distinction of the lecturer attracted many, and this continued to be the case with the Sidgwick Memorial Lecture. A student of natural science has expressed her deep debt to the attraction to good literature which these lectures afforded. Latterly the lectures given by holders of the new professorship of English (Dr. Verrall and Sir A. Quiller Couch), which are open to other than special students of the subject, amply provided for the objects aimed at in the earlier Newnham lectures.

Naturally the societies or clubs that loom largest in the life of present and the memories of past students are those connected with games. Hockey, as already said, was started by the first Principal herself, and it has remained for a long time one of the most prominent of the games societies. The several Halls have their teams, and play against one another; the College team plays against Girton and more distant colleges and schools as well as other clubs; also matches are played between past and present students. Fives is provided for by good courts. Cricket is played in the summer term. Tennis had been with us from the beginning of Lawn Tennis itself, and ash courts made the game possible all the year round. Lacrosse was introduced a good deal later. The introduction of bicycling during the middle nineties furnished a new mode of exercise and stimulated exploration of the country.

There have been, of course, many smaller societies: Sharp Practice, to make students ready in debate; boating, which has recently arrived at having an eight of its own ; others of names incomprehensible to any but the initiated. In connection with the Women's Settlement in Southwark, there has from its beginning been a society following its progress and contributing to its funds. The visits of Residents in the Settlement to explain to the students their work or some branch of it have been very interesting occasions—especially in the days when Miss Gladstone was Warden, and came to give a humorous account of her experiences, professedly to the first-year students, practically to as many of the students and staff as could crowd into the room.

Although there has not been till lately a formal dramatic society, any dramatic talent among the students has generally revealed itself fairly soon. The excuse of some worthy object to be served by threepenny tickets has been made the occasion of extremely lively impromptu performances. Especially the gift for melodrama has been displayed with success and has often caused intense amusement. More serious plays, or scenes from plays, have been exhibited from time to time, but those have been most successful which had the least elaborate preparation. It may be mentioned that Newnham students have taken part in serious dramatic performances organized by members of the University ; as in the *Comus*, acted on the occasion of the Miltonic Tercentenary.

I

In other fields there has been collective activity
among Newnham students. There have been
various religious societies, in most of which Newnham students are combined with those of Girton
and other Colleges. In Newnham itself there have
been societies for reading and discussing religious
and moral questions on Sunday evenings, the
subjects being sometimes theoretical, sometimes
practical. There has been a branch of a Church
Society called " The Society of the Annunciation,"
which had corporate Communion with Girton and
some religious addresses in a Cambridge church.
But far the largest and most influential is the
Student Christian Movement, which has arisen from
small beginnings and now has vigorous branches all
over the world. Connected with this there has
always been a collective and particular effort
towards missionary work. A good many Newnham
students became Student Volunteers, and some are
doing excellent work abroad, especially in schools
and Colleges of a new type, requiring higher education, and in medical practice. But the operation of
the whole movement is too well known to need
description here. It has branched out into new
departments, and has changed both its qualifications for membership and its relations to religious
bodies at home and abroad, so as to become a far
more potent agency than formerly in all Colleges
and among varied types of student. Some of its

leaders are frequently in Cambridge, and are cordially received at Newnham as well as in the Cambridge Colleges generally.

With regard to students and the political world. There had been a Suffrage Society in the College from comparatively early times. It has already been noticed how there had been among the early promoters of higher education for women a good many who set great hopes on the improvement of the position of women as citizens, and especially on their acquisition of the parliamentary vote. There were, however, among Staff and students of Newnham, several who felt much disgusted with the lawlessness and general want of reason and sobriety with which, in some quarters, the political cause of women was associated. A few, on the other hand, though not among those in authority, were inclined to go great lengths against the injustice and levity with which the whole question was treated by Parliament and by the Government. Those who desired and believed in the suffrage, but strongly disapproved of the violent and illegal actions of the extreme wing, took an active part in the orderly demonstrations organised by the law-abiding section of the movement. Thus members of the Staff and of the student body walked in the London processions and took part in the " Pilgrimage " of June 1912. A very small number of former students carried their principles to the extreme and suffered in consequence. But the attitude in general of Newnham in the whole matter was one of decided conviction, combined with patience and moderation.

Perhaps a few words should be said here as to the changes which were made, or gradually came about, in the necessary rules for student life and behaviour. It must always be remembered that fifty years ago, both unreasoned etiquette and the opinions of reasonable men and women recognised much severer rules for the general conduct of young women than are in force to-day ; also that in Cambridge, so much a city of men, the standard of conventional propriety for women was stricter than in most other places. Miss Clough and her fellow workers in the early times were sometimes obliged, for the sake of security against prejudice and gossip, to walk very warily, always, however, avoiding the imposition of such restraints as would have impeded either good work or the enjoyment of good health. It has been seen how Miss Clough herself undertook the some-times weary duty of chaperoning and minimized its inconvenience, and in little restrictions of a social kind she tried to impress on the early students that they were guests of the University and also pioneers who might by their own behaviour improve or spoil the chances of more liberty for those who should come after. As time went on, many rules were relaxed, and those that now have to be observed are laid down with the utmost care by the authorities, special regard being paid to the opinions and counsel of those who have to maintain order and discipline in the University and the Colleges.

The students themselves have never been discouraged from presenting to the heads of their separate Halls or to the Principal any suggestions as to possible modifications in domestic arrangement or in general regulations. Machinery for this purpose has been devised and modified from time to time. The students in residence choose (since 1911) a Senior Student, and it is one of her duties to communicate their views to the authorities. A joint committee of staff and students deliberates upon proposed alterations. There is also a Hall senior student elected by each Hall separately. It is generally recognised that great care is still required in forbidding or sanctioning matters which to a newcomer seem much more simple than they really are. The past prosperity of the College has been in very great part due to a good understanding between governors and governed, and this is still, in a sense, to be regarded as the sheet anchor of the College in Cambridge. It seems to be recognised in the Colleges of the University that the only way to avoid excessive ebullitions of youthful spirit is to enlist on the side of law and order some popular and leading spirits among the undergraduates themselves. The same principle applies in women's Colleges, where the students, as a rule (like public schoolboys), have learned, in pre-college days, the necessity of rules and regularity. If Newnham ever becomes a College of the University, the students will, of course, be subjected to proctorial discipline, but the process would probably be found not to involve any conspicuous changes in College life.

EPILOGUE

1914 AND AFTER

THE outbreak of the Great War marks an epoch in the history of Newnham as of other institutions at home and abroad. Its experience confirms also the commonly repeated statement that in many things the results of the war have proved very different from those anticipated either in the event of success or of failure. One consequence confidently anticipated was at least temporary decline. We were bound to suffer restrictions and something of poverty, for the first item in which the so-called practical man and woman economize is education. Yet we all see at this moment that in spite of fiscal difficulties in public and losses in private affairs, all our schools and colleges are full to overflowing. Newnham participates in this experience, and is compelled to refuse promise of admission to many qualified and promising students. The reasons for this surprising fact are to be found partly in government policy, partly in economic causes still awaiting elucidation ; possibly also in a genuine belief in education as a good thing for women as for men.

135

One danger is to be apprehended : the lack of really well-prepared students, owing to the comparative scarcity of able University women who enter the teaching profession. Yet while these words are being written, the course of events may take an opposite trend. The salaries of mistresses in schools are raised to an unprecedented height, if perhaps hardly more than is required to cover increased cost of living. And the young women who have been serving the country in administrative work or directing their energies to the land or to domestic productiveness may, in course of time, find their way back to the task of teaching, which, after all, has inspired a genuine enthusiasm in many of our leaders. Early in the War, when some students were feeling doubts whether patriotic duty might not bid them give up their academic course for labour of a directly useful kind, the Right Hon. H. A. L. Fisher gave in Cambridge a convincing address as to the necessity of keeping up educational and academic work with a view to the requirements of the future.

Any even slight account of what Newnham students of past days did during the War would seem to be out of place here in that they did it as individuals, not as a College.[1] Collectively, however, they furnished, along with Girton, a hospital

[1] A list of the various war work of Newnham students in 1914-19 is in process of preparation.

unit which did excellent work in Belgium, France and Serbia, and later in Salonika. This unit was organized under Scottish management by the Union of Suffrage Societies, but there was, of course, no political aim in its operations.

Past students of Newnham were engaged in War Hospitals in many places. At the same time some of the most competent Newnham mathematicians were employed in making calculations to assist in the construction of aeroplanes. A multitude undertook work in helping soldiers' families, providing necessaries for hospitals, and housing refugees; while others went in companies to gather in fruit and do other work on the land. In London so many were engaged in government offices that a past student in London in the summer of 1917, meeting College friends at every turn, would salute each fresh face with : " What department are you in ? " Many took temporary posts in Universities and boys' schools. Those who remained in Cambridge had much to do in teaching English to Belgians, Serbians and other refugees, and in visiting wounded soldiers in the First Eastern and other Hospitals.

The result of all this activity along unexpectedly opened lines cannot yet be estimated. Certainly proof was given of the efficiency of educated women in carrying on work that had never been open to them before. In some regions (e.g. that of police work) it has been agreed upon that even in normal times it is highly desirable that some women should be employed. The issue must be awaited in patience.

It would, of course, be unworthy of the College to suppose that in their activities these women were moved by a wish to better their position and that of their College. Common humanity and genuine patriotism were at the bottom of their efforts. But doubtless the capacity and energy which they displayed helped indirectly towards the grant of the Suffrage. It is a very notable thing that when the Suffrage came, past students of Newnham and Girton of the qualified age, who had the " equivalent of a degree," were adjudged capable of using the parliamentary vote for the University of Cambridge. Parliament was, however, not so liberal as Dublin had been, as it did not recognise as " equivalent " the Tripos Certificates given before the Graces of 1881.

One more change awaited the College at the end of the last academic year, in the retirement of the Principal, Miss Katharine Stephen, a loss much deplored, though Miss Stephen retains her seat on the Council. Her devotion to the work she had undertaken, and the ability with which she discharged it need no eulogies here. Happily, her place has been filled by the niece and biographer of the First Principal. Miss B. A. Clough has not only

MISS B. A. CLOUGH.

spent many years within the College precincts and watched its continuous progress, with occasional drawbacks, from comparatively early days ; she has also been intimately associated with its pioneers and has acquired an unrivalled knowledge of the aspirations and the needs of student life. As, in old times, the rule of a Foundress Abbess seemed sometimes to be best carried on by a niece who had lived much in her environment, so we may hope good things in future from the fact that our Principal is in more than name the honoured successor of Anne Jemima Clough.

As these chapters were being written, the struggle was again begun for membership in the University of Cambridge, and—as we know only too well—the result was a failure, though not so crushing a failure as the attempt in 1897 when the demands were far more modest. It is not desirable to dwell on this event, but we hope we may accept the assurance of many friends that it cannot be long before we obtain what we are asking. Meanwhile we may console ourselves by thinking that the Women's Colleges have earned the respect even of opponents, and that there is no probability of their being deprived of the privileges which they still enjoy. It would be unwise to pretend indifference to our defeat. Yet we have full reason to celebrate our Jubilee in joy and hope. For, after all, the treasure to seek which our pioneers

came to Cambridge fifty years ago, is in our posses-
sion and likely to remain with us permanently.
That treasure is Education : the opportunity of
learning from the best teachers ; of co-operation
with like-minded learners ; the opening up of
opportunities of learning more of nature and of
man ; fitness for doing whatever tasks the future
may offer to those who seek, like our first benefactors, a life of active and intelligent service.
That was their ideal and it may well continue
to be ours.

INDEX

GLASGOW: PRINTED AT THE UNIVERSITY PRESS BY ROBERT MACLEHOSE AND CO. LTD.